THE Effective School Leader's Guide TO Management

To my children, Mark and Joel,
Their partners, Shannon and Molly
And my wonderful granddaughters, Audrey and Stella

JANE L. SIGFORD

THE Effective School Leader's Guide TO Management

CORWIN PRESS
A SAGE Publications Company
Thousand Oaks, California

For information:

Corwin Press
A Sage Publications Company
2455 Teller Road
Thousand Oaks, California 91320
www.corwinpress.com

Sage Publications Ltd.
1 Oliver's Yard
55 City Road
London EC1Y 1SP
United Kingdom

Sage Publications India Pvt. Ltd.
B-42, Panchsheel Enclave
New Delhi 110 017 India

Printed in the United States of America

Library of Congress Cataloging-in-Publication Data

Sigford, Jane L.
The effective school leader's guide to management / Jane L. Sigford.
    p. cm.
Includes bibliographical references and index.
ISBN 1-4129-1758-1 (cloth) — ISBN 1-4129-1759-X (pbk.)
   1. School management and organization—United States—Handbooks, manuals, etc. 2. Educational leadership—United States—Handbooks, manuals, etc. I. Title.
LB2805.S542 2006
371.2—dc22   2005014815

This book is printed on acid-free paper.

05   06   07   08   09   10   9   8   7   6   5   4   3   2   1

Acquisitions Editor:	Elizabeth Brenkus
Editorial Assistant:	Candice L. Ling
Production Editor:	Diane S. Foster
Copy Editor:	Sarah Blackmon
Typesetter:	C&M Digitals (P) Ltd.
Proofreader:	Penny Sippel
Indexer:	Judy Hunt
Cover Designer:	Rose Storey
Graphic Designer:	Scott Van Atta

Contents

Preface

There is an old Chinese curse, "May you live in interesting times." Current school leaders may feel that we are living in those times. We have increasing pressures on schools that keep education on top of political agendas. Newspapers report on how well—or not—schools and states are working to close the achievement gap. Critics state we must educate all students for the 21st century, whatever that means, because we must remain competitive in the global workplace to develop well-educated workers who are creative and work well in groups. Our school populations reflect the increasingly diverse general populations. Schools are criticized as being unfriendly to boys. Letting some students "slip through the cracks" can no longer be acceptable. However, methods and practices that used to work may no longer satisfy the needs of the varied populations we serve. In addition, since September 11, 2001, all of these agendas must be accomplished in most states with diminished resources.

Authors such as Michael Fullan, Stephen Covey, Jim Collins, Richard DuFour, Douglas Reeves, and Margaret Wheatley, among many others, write about the type of leadership that is necessary to accomplish these Herculean tasks in our contemporary schools. We can read about instructional leaders, visionary leaders, leaders in a professional learning community, and "Level 5 Leaders." No one disagrees that leadership is important. However, there is no one theory or method that works with every leader. In fact, two people may adhere to the same philosophical viewpoint of leadership and exhibit different degrees of success, depending on the climate of the school where they practice.

To make leadership happen, whatever style of leadership it may be, it is necessary to know more than theories. It is important to understand history, politics, and human behavior, as well. Even destructive leaders, such as Saddam Hussein and Hitler, had to understand how to put all the pieces together to create a culture, whereby they could accomplish their goals. Leadership is a blend of the visionary and the mundane, the prophet and the maintenance worker, and the salesperson and the consumer.

It is easier to develop a theory about leadership than it is to put that same theory into practice.

What part of leadership are the day-to-day management strategies that keep an organization running smoothly so that leadership can take place? Leadership also requires successful management. Graduate programs and seminars expose students to theories and ideas about effective leaders, but they seldom address the more commonplace aspects of how to put all the pieces together into effective management practices. Do we mistakenly believe that effective management strategies will just fall into place?

A leader cannot truly lead unless the elements of successful management also take place. Therefore, this book provides strategies of day-to-day management so that the educational leader has more time to practice educational leadership.

What makes this book different from other books is that it addresses leadership and management together. The book functions as a handbook for the new administrator and practicing administrator alike by providing strategies and resources based on research and cumulative years of experience.

Management and leadership are interwoven, much like a wall hanging consists of warp and woof weaves. Warp describes the longitudinal threads and woof is the name for the horizontal fill threads. Individually each thread may be beautiful, but it is just that, a thread. Many threads woven together create something new, because the synergy of the individual threads with their different colors, textures, and tension creates an entirely new object, a cloth, if you will.

Management and leadership are like the warp and woof weaves of a cloth. Leadership is like the longitudinal threads and management is the fill. Together they create something richer and more complex than the individual strands. Each of the threads—each chapter in this book—interweaves to create a piece that has a synergy that is greater than the sum of its parts. The book as a whole creates a new interaction among the pieces.

This book has four goals: First, its purpose is to act as a handbook containing an overview of the many individual components of school leadership that are normally scattered among many textbooks and resources. Second, if more in-depth study is needed of any one topic, suggested resources are provided. Third, there are individual reflection questions, under the heading "Personal Journal," for personal use as one reads the book. Fourth, group discussion questions are provided to facilitate professional development discussions, particularly among a group of peers.

The book is designed to provide an overview in one place of the key topics in the daily life of an administrator. The chapters are designed to provide a basic understanding with the recognition that many, many books have been written about each topic. If someone needs more information about any one topic, resources are provided. The leader must be both a generalist and specialist. Putting all the major topics in one book provides a starting point for new administrators. It will also help someone to understand the complexity and interlocking parts and knowledge that are demanded of contemporary school leaders.

Another important reason for the book is to look at the management side of leadership. The most knowledgeable person in the world about leadership theories may not be an effective school leader if that person is unable to figure out how to build a master schedule, keep the buses running on time, and maintain a safe school. Those are management pieces.

We do not spend enough time with new administrators, in particular, helping them to put all the pieces together so that the school can run effectively and allow instruction to take place.

The book has a whole-to-part organization. It begins with an overall discussion of the major discussion of leadership and management in Chapter 1. Chapters 2 through 11 discuss topical items in a fashion that integrates management with leadership. Practical ideas are offered from the management perspective to deal with the more ethereal concepts of leadership. Chapters 12 through 14 take the topics to a very personal, reflective level for each individual to examine how they can take the big ideas of leadership and management and think about them from a topical perspective. They ask the individual to relate from a very personal, introspective frame.

Acknowledgments

Corwin Press gratefully acknowledges the contributions of the following individuals:

Bea Lingenfelter
Assistant Professor
Benerd School of Education
University of the Pacific
Stockton, CA

Mark Merrell
Principal
James Madison High School
Vienna, VA

Bob Moore
Superintendent
Oklahoma City Public Schools
Oklahoma City, OK

About the Author

 **Jane L. Sigford** is currently the Executive Director of Curriculum and Instruction for the Wayzata Public Schools in Wayzata, Minnesota, a suburb of Minneapolis. Prior to this she has been a high school principal in a suburban high school, an assistant principal at an urban high school in St. Paul, Minnesota, a dean of students, an English teacher, a special education teacher, and a staff development trainer. She also helped create a drop-in center for divergent learners at a suburban high school.

She has been an adjunct professor for the University of St. Thomas and Hamline University, both in St. Paul, Minnesota. She has a B.S. degree in English from Bemidji State University, Bemidji, Minnesota. Her master's degree from San Diego State University is in English, with a concentration on black literature. Her certifications in teaching students with learning disabilities and in teaching students with emotional/behavioral disabilities are from the University of St. Thomas, St. Paul, Minnesota. She obtained her doctorate degree in educational policy and administration from the University of Minnesota, Minneapolis.

She is the proud mother of two adult sons and a proud mother-in-law as well. She is grateful for being part of the lives of her two granddaughters, Audrey and Stella, who give her great joy.

Her email address is jlsigford@comcast.net.

PART I

Introduction

1

Leadership and Management

Creating a Professional Learning Community

As I waited for my chicken sandwich and fries, I watched the manager of the local McDonald's shout out orders. "I'm waiting for five fries. We're behind. Pick it up! Pick it up!" This man would not have succeeded as the principal in a school. He was using management strategies expected within his organization, but I doubt if anyone would have described him as a leader.

McDonald's needs managers, but schools need leaders who have effective management skills and strategies. What is the difference between a manager and a leader? What is the difference between management and leadership?

In a recent article in *The School Administrator*, John Forsyth stated, "Effective superintendents are identified as key to the success of improvement efforts" (2004, p. 6). Research supports that effective schools have "good central-office leadership and sound school board governance" (2005, p. 7).

Valerie Chrisman, in her article "How Schools Sustain Success" (2005), stated "when asked to list three factors that were most likely to improve test scores, surveyed principals from both successful and unsuccessful schools included district leadership. All the unsuccessful sample schools demonstrated a lack of strong district leadership" (p. 18).

We also know that schools that have high academic achievement have instructional leaders as principals. Forsyth stated, "The importance of the principal cannot be overstated" (2005, p. 7). According to Elaine McEwan, in her book *10 Traits of Highly Effective Principals* (2003), "school leadership occasionally disappears from the radar screen of educational reform" (p. xxi). However, with the push from the No Child Left Behind Act, "Policy makers have discovered that teachers, tests, and textbooks can't produce results *without* highly effective principals to facilitate, model, *and* lead (p. xxiii).

It would be a powerful research topic to look at the interplay and synergistic effects of building and district leadership. We seem to study one or the other, but not the interplay among them. Do buildings make as much progress if those in the district central office are not perceived as strong educational leaders? Is there a compounding effect in districts with instructional leaders at the district and building levels? Can strong district leadership inspire academic achievement without having strong instructional building leaders? One wonders . . .

Leadership Is . . .

Literature about leadership does two things. First, it describes leadership as an entity. Second, it describes the traits of leaders. We will look at leadership first.

What is leadership? Theories of instructional leadership abound. Richard DuFour, author of *Professional Learning Communities at Work: Best Practices for Enhancing Student Achievement* (1998), said, "Research of effective schools from the 1970s and 1980s placed principals at the head of school improvement efforts" (p. 183). Leadership creates a shared mission and values among the staff, collaborative teams, action orientation and experimentation, continuous improvement, and results orientation (pp. 25–28).

Terrence E. Deal and Kent D. Peterson, in *Shaping School Culture: The Heart of Leadership* (1999), described the heart of leadership as the ability to read school culture, strengthen it, and change or shape it for a new direction, if necessary. They talk about the importance of symbolic leaders who understand the roles of poets, historians, visionaries, anthropological sleuths, symbols, potters, actors, and healers (pp. 85–99). Notice that many of these roles have strong affective components.

Thomas Sergiovanni, in *The Lifeworld of Leadership* (2000), describes it as "special leadership because they [the schools] are lifeworld intensive. Values play a particularly important role" (p. 166).

In a report on "Leadership for Student Learning," the National Association of Secondary School Principals (NASSP) stated that the leadership exhibited by 21st century principals will need to be

- Instructional—focusing on teaching and learning, professional development, data-driven decision making and accountability
- Community—being aware of the school's role in the greater society, with shared leadership among educators, community partners, and residents; close relations with parents and others; and advocacy for school capacity, building, and resources
- Visionary—demonstrating energy, commitment, entrepreneurial spirit, values, and conviction that all children will learn at high levels, as well as inspiring others with this vision both inside and outside the school building (p. 8). http://www.iel .org/programs/21st/reports/principal.pdf

In his Pulitzer Prize and National Book Award winning book entitled *Leadership* (1978), James MacGregor Burns hoped that the secret of leadership was "that people can be lifted into their better selves" (p. 462). Yet "to understand the nature of leadership requires understanding of the essence of power, for leadership is a special form of power" (p. 12). Though we would like to use that power for good purposes, not all leadership is positive. We have seen leadership throughout the course of history that has also been negative and harmful. However, this book will only address leadership and leaders who move learning institutions in positive directions.

Peter Senge, in *Schools That Learn* (2000), titled the chapter on leadership as "Leading Without Control." His leadership has the following characteristics:

- Engagement—the ability to recognize the complexity of systems and facilitate reflective conversations about difficult issues
- Systems thinking—the ability to "recognize the hidden dynamics of complex systems and to find leverage" (p. 415)
- Leading learning—modeling "learner-centered" as opposed to "authority-centered" inside and outside the classroom (p. 416)
- Self-awareness—understanding the impact decisions have on people and the ability to reflect and establish one's personal vision (p. 418)

Leadership is dynamic, process-oriented, and personally engaged. One type of leadership that we are particularly interested in, instructional leadership, is that "strong leadership [which] promotes excellence and equity in education and entrails projecting, promoting, and holding steadfast to the vision; garnering and allocating resources; communicating progress; and supporting the people, programs, services, and activities implemented to achieve the school's vision" according to Sally J. Zepeda in *The Principal as Instructional Leader* (2003).

The National Association of Secondary School Principals issued a document, *Breaking Ranks II: Strategies for Leading High School Reform*, in 2004. The document is seen as a footprint in how to reshape high schools to meet the needs of the 21st century. One topic, of course, is leadership. The document analyzed three familiar types of leadership: one, visionary, which views change as necessary but may be overly optimistic and not thoughtful in preplanning analysis; two, technocratic leadership, which emphasizes quantifiable results while neglecting the concerns of the people involved creating short-term gains at the risk of long-term resentment; and three, sympathetic leadership, which focuses on people but may neglect the quantifiable results (p. 21). In contrast, effective leadership would be that which "looks outward to diagnose needs, challenges beliefs and assumptions, shapes a vision over time, and maintains persistence (p. 22).

Ethics and Spirituality of Leadership

Lately, there has been more discussion in the literature about the ethics and spirituality of leadership. Corporate scandals have brought the discussion to the front page of the newspapers, particularly for the business sector. We have heard about Enron and Martha Stewart and have watched as Stewart came home from her stint in prison, vowing to rise again. In addition, there have been discussions about ethics and moral purpose in education as well. Paul Houston, executive director of American Association of School Administrators (AASA), wrote, "But educational leaders, because of their responsibility for the future through touching the lives of children, have an even greater obligation" (School Administrator, 2002, p. 6). Our mission is greater because we work with children, and to be moral and ethical adults, we need to teach and model such behavior. "We get our work done, not through mandate and fiat, but by gathering folks together and persuading them to do what is right" (p. 8). Our obligation is not merely teaching the 3 R's; it is to respond to the need to lead in a fashion that provides an ethical example.

Sergiovanni (2000) believes that school leadership is "at root, . . . an ethical science concerned with good or better processes, good or better means, and good or better ends. This immersion of schooling and of school administration in values, preferences, ideas, aspirations, and hopes accentuates the importance of lifeworld concerns of local schools and their constituents. To be ethically responsive the school leader must be vigilant in protecting the lifeworld from being colonized by the systemsworld" (p. 166).

Deepak Chopra, author and motivational speaker, wrote in *The School Administrator*, September 2002. He described an ethical leadership as a system where

- Leaders and followers co-create each other.
- Leadership is a symbolic soul of the group. The leader allows the individuals and organization to grow from inside out.
- Inner qualities determine the results. The vision is only as good as the inner qualities of those carrying it out.
- A multitude of responses are available because the leader must understand the mixture and contradictions of possible responses—fight/flight, creativity/boredom, etc.
- Leaders give of themselves.
- A leader must be comfortable with disorder (pp. 11–12).

Dr. Michael Hartoonian, senior fellow in the Department of Educational Policy & Administration at the University of Minnesota, Minneapolis, would take the responsibility of ethical and moral leadership of public education even further. He stated that "a democratic free market cannot function, nor can commerce flourish, without quality infrastructures to help establish an ethical, aesthetic, efficient, and healthy context for business. The public school is the essential element for the preservation and enhancement of both democracy and the free market. But this can only happen if we understand that public schools were not created primarily to serve the private interests of students and their parents. Public schools exist for the wider community. They are here for the common good—to establish the intellectual, ethical, and aesthetic infrastructure for democracy and capitalism" (unpublished speech, MASA, April 21, 2005).

That means that schools have a "civic purpose" that must honor what he calls "the common good." We must think about others, our responsibility to society in our country and world. "Schools must critically serve a public purpose—to enhance the public realm that is the economic, ethical, and aesthetic infrastructure." "An education must be earned through good habits and rightful behavior. It comes from practicing work ethic and intellectual virtue and from recognizing that individuals have duties not only to themselves, and to one another, but to the common good as well. If our public schools are to take their rightful and essential place in the republic, then the culture must understand that without a conception of the common good, public school makes no sense" (Unpublished speech, April 21, 2005).

The discussion about the moral and ethical responsibility of leadership and leaders is an important one. Because our work is so culture-laden, we who are responsible for leadership must take our responsibilities seriously if we are to continue to have leadership in our country that is truly bound by doing "the right thing." We affect all of our children who grow up to be the adults that exhibit leadership across professions. It is incumbent upon us to have discussions about and to be examples of ethical leadership.

Leaders Have . . .

Other literature on leadership describes leaders. Gene E. Hall and Shirley M. Hord, in *Change in Schools: Facilitating the Process* (1987), stated that "the leadership literature has in large measure centered on the analysis of the traits, behaviors, or styles brought to the role of leader and on the extent to which the situation influences leadership potential" (p. 51). As one reads about the traits leaders have, it is important to note that the lists are often a mix of personal traits and skill sets. It is an important topic for future discussion to analyze how it would be possible to train administrators to have leadership skills when some of the traits are more about the person than about the respective skill sets they possess.

Daniel Goleman, Co-director of the Consortium for Research on Emotional Intelligence in Organizations at Rutgers University, discussed leaders in terms of emotional intelligence. In 2002, Goleman et al., in *Primal Leadership: Realizing the Power of Emotional Intelligence*, said simply, "Great leaders move us" (p. 3). The ability to do so, he said, is that "no matter what leaders set out to do . . . their success depends on how they do it. Great leadership works through the emotions" (p. 3).

In *Good to Great* (2001), Jim Collins, dubbed his top leaders as "Level 5 Leaders" and described them as people who

- Demonstrate a paradoxical mix of personal humility and professional will
- Set up successors to be successful also
- Display compelling modesty and are understated
- Are fanatically driven to produce sustained results
- Are more plow horse than show horse
- Attribute much of success to good luck rather than to personal greatness

- Use window and mirror approach—when there is success, they use a window to see factors other than themselves for success. When improvement is needed, they use a mirror to look for ways to improve (pp. 39–40).

The Level 5 leader uses skills to put together many components to "manage the system," not the people (p. 125). In other words, leadership allows the leader to concentrate on the synergy of the system, rather than on the components themselves. The school leader is not like the McDonald's manager who is on the food line calling for more French fries. Instead, the leader is putting together the components so that the employees themselves are monitoring output and input. "Leadership is influence" (Reeves, 2004, p. 25).

Traits of an Effective School Principal

Therefore, what does leadership look like specifically in the context of education? What are the traits of a principal as leader?

Based on research and interviews with 108 individuals, Elaine McEwan assembled what she called *10 Traits of Highly Effective Principals: From Good to Great Performance* (2003). An effective principal has the following traits in various degrees: Communicator, Educator, Envisioner, Facilitator, Change Master, Culture Builder, Activator, Producer, Character Builder, and Contributor. According to McEwan, no one person is perfect in all traits, but "[the principals] are all works in progress" (p. xvi).

McEwan believed that some traits were more dominant than others but that an effective leader *must* possess all of the traits "in some measure to be effective" (p. xxix). In her work, there were three major trait areas: "communication, instruction, and sense of purpose and mission" (p. xxv). "The respondents believed that highly effective principals were mission-driven individuals with strong communication skills, a high level of knowledge about teaching and learning, and the ability to provide instructional leadership" (p. xxvii). At the opposite end of the spectrum, "only about 10 percent of the respondents believed that highly effective principals should be *take-charge* individuals . . . and only one vote was cast for *charismatic principals*" (p. xxvi). This work corroborates the findings of Jim Collins's *Good to Great* when he said, "The moment a leader allows himself to become the primary reality people worry about, rather than reality being the primary reality, you have a recipe for mediocrity, or worse. This is one of the key reasons why less charismatic leaders often produce better long-term results than their more charismatic counterparts" (p. 72).

Cynthia D. McCauley (1990), Director of Education and Nonprofit Sector Research Group, prepared a report for the Center for Creative Leadership on the traits of an effective school principal. She conducted a mega-analysis of five high-quality research studies to derive Competencies of Effective Principals. Following is a list reflecting this research:

- *Beliefs and Values About Education.* Effective principals are guided by a well-developed philosophy of education. They focus on providing the best educational experiences for students. They have high expectations of students, teachers, and self.
- *Cognitive Maps of Factors Influencing Schooling.* Broad, multifaceted knowledge of what factors inside and outside of the school have an impact on student learning. This knowledge is derived from personal experience, professional judgment, and research findings.
- *Information Processing and Decision-Making Styles.* Effective principals are systematic information gatherers and manipulators. They anticipate problems and are decisive. They seek input and involvement from others in making decisions.
- *Setting Direction.* Effective principals are active in setting school priorities and direction. They combine district goals with their own school needs in setting priorities.
- *Organizing and Implementing.* Effective principals develop ways and means for reaching goals. They establish procedures for handling routine matters. They clearly delegate authority and responsibility and serve as role models for how to get things done.
- *Monitoring.* Effective principals monitor progress toward goals and evaluate staff systematically, feeding back the information gained.
- *Communicating.* Effective principals express ideas clearly and frequently.
- *Developing Staff.* Effective principals identify staff developmental needs and work to improve the staff in these areas.
- *Managing Relationships.* Effective principals develop productive relationships with their staff and work to resolve conflict. They are aware of the needs, concerns, and feelings of others. They make themselves available to staff and are honest and direct with staff. They also maintain positive relations with students and with the community.
- *Adapting Actions to Context.* Effective principals tailor leadership styles to fit the situation and adapt behaviors to fit the

organizational and community context of their schools (p. 10). In addition, principals need to have competencies in school-based management, teacher empowerment, and working with stakeholders (pp. 11–13).

Todd Whitaker (2003) studied 50 schools to write a book, *What Great Principals Do Differently*, describing the difference between more effective and less effective principals. His characteristics were derived by analyzing how great principals focused their attention, how they spent their time and energy, and what guided their decisions. What he learned was that "it is never about programs; it is always about people" (p. 8).

According to DuFour and Eaker (1998), effective school leaders

- Lead through shared vision and values rather than through rules and procedures.
- Involve faculty members in school's decision-making process and empower individuals to act.
- Provide staff with the information, training, and parameters they need to make a good decision. (pp. 184–187)

In addition to the litany of traits already described, this author believes that effective school leaders also demonstrate the following:

- *Knowledge.* A leader must pursue knowledge in a variety of topics as a lifelong learner. An effective leader is intelligent, well read, and, most importantly, inquisitive.
- *Process Skill.* A leader understands the stages of process, the stages of change, the process of learning, and the process of human development, to name a few.
- *Awareness/intuition.* A leader must be aware of nuances, body language, culture, disruptions, feelings, tones, and bad days. Whether this is intuition, or keen insight, does not matter. What matters is that a leader pays attention to the emotional, non-verbal aspects of the human dimension.
- *Kindness.* A leader must be able to feel empathy. Without it, there is no understanding of the human condition.
- *Sense of Humor.* To have a sense of humor, one must understand irony and paradox. Humor helps one appreciate the idiosyncrasies of life. But most important, it helps keep a balance between the real and surreal, important and unimportant, tragic and comic.
- *Reflection.* A leader must be a reflective practitioner. Parker Palmer, author of *The Courage to Teach* (1998), put it this way.

"... teaching [leadership] holds a mirror to the soul. If I am willing to look at that mirror, and not run from what I see, I have a chance to gain self-knowledge, and knowing myself is as crucial to good teaching [leading] as knowing my students and my subject" (p. 2).

- *Understanding of Paradox.* Whatever lesson or process we are engaged in will have an opposite that can teach a valuable lesson. The key is to pay attention. Nature is a prime example of paradox because as winter comes, plants start preparing for spring by storing energy. We do not see the hidden preparation, much as we do not see the hidden lessons in what we are doing unless we pay attention.
- *Management Knowledge.* A school leader needs to be able to use management strategies to allow leadership to come to fruition.

Management Is . . .

We have discussed leadership and leaders. What is the difference between that and management? How must an educational leader also be a manager?

A manager is someone who organizes the daily life of an organization so that it runs smoothly. A manager needs to understand the interaction of the physical plant and the physical needs of the people within the organization. In schools, management involves such things as designing an effective master schedule, organizing the buses so they run on time, or making certain that food service is well-designed and efficient. Management is also knowing how to manage time, how to multitask when necessary, how to respond to parent concerns, and how to evaluate teachers in a timely fashion. On a personal level, it is the ability for an individual to manage time to answer messages, to submit budget proposals on time, to utilize clerical help, and yet to have time to be an instructional leader and remain mentally, physically, and spiritually healthy.

In our training programs, we often discuss the management pieces as a stepchild when we are learning about the more glorious aspects of theories about leadership and leaders. We may practice in-box activities to help learn to prioritize daily events. We may take a seminar in time management. However, we do not spend time talking about the need for integrating management skills with leadership skills as keys to being an effective school leader.

Businesses talk about management, particularly about time management, as though that makes a person a better leader. Stephen

Covey, in *First Things First* (1994), did a meta-analysis of time management literature and described eight basic approaches. Six pertinent strategies are discussed here.

1. *Get Organized.* There is a belief that having enough file drawers or bins or calendars will help make a person more efficient and will prevent wasting time looking for misplaced items. The weakness is, however, that the organizing "becomes an end in itself, rather than a means to greater ends" (p. 323). This management tactic supports the belief that an efficient manager has a clean and orderly desk. A clean desk is only that—a clean desk. It does not indicate a person's leadership or management capabilities.

2. *Warrior Approach.* The warrior approach demands that a person protect time to focus on important tasks only. This approach does strengthen the belief in personal responsibility for how a person spends one's time. However, it also puts managers into a "survivalist paradigm," to "put up barriers, say no" (p. 324).

3. *Goal Approach.* Broadly, this approach says to know what the goal is and focus all efforts toward that goal. One strength of this approach is to help people set goals. A weakness, however, is that sometimes the goal is impossible to achieve, which may or may not be the individual's responsibility. Another weakness is that the goal may not bring the expected or desired outcome, which feels defeating.

4. *Prioritization and Values Identification.* This technique involves values clarification and task ranking. However, again natural laws may interfere with the completion of the tasks and sometimes values have to change. Personal values may not be in sync with those of the organization and may not bring success or happiness.

5. *Magic Tool Approach.* The magic tool approach is much like the magic curriculum approach. If only we had the right math curriculum, all learners would learn. If only we had the right tool—computer software, calendar program, filing system—then the person would be an effective leader or manager. However, there is no perfect tool. Sometimes the tool becomes rigid. And sometimes it takes more time—to write everything down, to use a color-coded system—than is necessary. Looking organized is not the same thing as *being* organized.

6. *Time Management 101.* There are often seminars available for one day experiences that give people kitschy ways to manage time. The weakness is again that not every strategy fits every learner. Such courses do not train people to develop their own best practices.

Purpose of Management

It is important to put management skills into a context. If the above management strategies are taught in isolation and not within a context of how effective management facilitates leadership or how certain strategies can help an effective leader, then the management strategies do not support or sustain leadership and leaders. If, however, successful management is strategically integrated into leadership, then the leader is able to cause leadership to happen.

Leadership and management must work together under the guiding hand of an ethical leader. Michael Fullan (2002), professor and author of many books on change and leadership, believes that "in a real sense we are talking about transforming the teaching profession . . ." (p. 14). Leaders exhibit interpersonal skills in a manner that demonstrates respect, understanding, empathy, and ethics in a context that is rich in paradox, messy in its human interactions, and beautiful in that we have the supreme gift of working with the children of our future. We have the opportunity to create and make a difference unlike any other profession.

How to Use Theory About Leadership and Management

As we study theories, whether they are about leadership, leaders, or management, it is important to make use of the theory. In graduate classes it is assumed that knowledge of theory will lead to better practice.

There are two ways to use theory. One, a person may look at theory from a macro perspective. What does this theory tell me about the big picture? About looking at systems? Some big ideas are helpful in examining a system of one particular job but may not be at all helpful in another situation. For example, a middle school principal was hired to create change in a system that was unhealthy and stuck. She had to use many of the strategies that are helpful in creating discomfort or cognitive dissonance. She had to be comfortable with the change process and the time it takes to make change occur. She applied the big ideas as relevant to change leadership (Sigford, 1995, p. 76).

In her next position, she was the principal of a middle school that was staffed by teachers who were determined to work together to create a learning environment for all students. This position needed her to be a good communicator, especially a good listener, and to facilitate the good ideas that teachers brought forward. It was her task to find resources in professional development, time and money to let the wonderful teachers do their job. Those two situations demanded very different leadership skills. She had to be very aware of the difference in systems and to apply different theoretical models as appropriate. She had to be able to look at both systems from a macro perspective and use tools that applied to each situation.

Another way to use theory is to identify an area for further study as a personal professional growth goal. For example, in looking at McEwan's (2003) traits of effective principals, Bill recognized that he needed to spend more time in being a "Culture Builder" in his building. According to McEwan (2003), a Culture Builder is one who understands and appreciates the power of culture, knows what a good culture looks like, facilitates development of core values, communicates those values clearly, rewards those who support and enhance the culture, builds cultures that people choose, and knows that the "small stuff" is really the "big stuff" (p. 101).

Bill is a high school principal of the "old school" who was a social studies teacher, a coach, and who has been a high school principal for a long time. However, leadership needs have changed over the past five years, particularly with No Child Left Behind. There is more need for data-driven decisions, which demand a better knowledge and utilization of technology. Also the culture of his building needs some attention in order to be effective and support the needs of the staff as they look at teaching increasingly diverse populations.

Bill decided that a personal and professional goal for him this year would be to work with a facilitator to research the core values of the staff and begin to build upon them. Another choice was that he read *Courage to Teach* by Parker Palmer (1998) and establish a discussion group with his teacher leader group. He recognized that he needed to channel his energies into new areas in order to respond to the different cultural needs of the building.

In addition to looking at leadership theory and individual traits, leaders also need to look at effective management skills in order to maximize the leadership potential. The McDonald's manager must make certain that the store has adequate supplies, labor, accounting systems, and clean bathrooms and tables. The manager must ensure that the bills are paid and that the parking lot is clean. Plus, there has to be enough ketchup.

School leaders must also attend to the management aspects. They can look at management from the macro perspective and from the personal, goal-setting perspective. For example, as a principal, I know that I do not pay enough attention to the custodial aspects of the building. It can be a goal of mine in the upcoming year to learn the intricacies of building maintenance and then work on facilitating good plant management. It cannot be stressed enough that an effective leader also has effective management strategies.

Therefore, the educational leader must look at theory and try to integrate the theories into the best practice, either from a big picture or by using ideas to fine tune daily practice.

No Such Thing as Perfection . . . Or the Human Element

If we have so many theories on leadership, leaders, and we know successful management techniques, why isn't every organization perfect? Why do we still struggle with defining and describing leadership? Why do we still offer management seminars?

Put very simply, it's because there is no such thing as a perfect theory, leader, situation, or implementation. No two people interpret theories the same, nor do they enact them the same. No two leaders have the same skill set. Plus, no two situations are the same. The role of the interaction of culture and leader cannot be underestimated. In addition, no two people exhibit the same management strengths and no two situations have exactly the same management needs.

Sergiovanni (2000) described it thus: "Schools also need special leadership because school professionals don't react warmly to the kind of hierarchically based command leadership or hero leadership that characterizes so many other kinds of organizations" (p. 166). "Ordinary images of how to organize, provide leadership and support, motivate, and ensure accountability just do not seem to fit schools very well" (p. 167). Because of that we keep trying new ideas, writing and reading new books, and tweaking old systems to try to make them better.

For example, I may feel that one of my greatest strengths is visionary leadership. I am able to see patterns and help move toward the future. However, if in a situation where the organization may be stuck and not wanting to move forward, I may not have the individual leader traits to move the organization along. However, in a different situation where the organization is ripe for vision, my theories and personal strengths may fit and I may be seen as a powerful educational leader.

Another graduate-school classmate, who sees himself as a strong organizational leader, who can put plans and designs into place, may not do well in an organization that needs vision and propelling into the future. Although we were in the same class and understand some of the same theories, we may have different levels of success based on the interaction of the culture of an organization, the application of theory, and the utilization of individual personal strengths and strategies. That's why it is much easier to write theories about leadership and leaders than it is to put those ideas into place in a manner that guarantees educational leadership and student achievement.

In addition, the concept of management weaves in and out of the discussion of leadership. If I am a strong visionary leader and cannot organize an effective master schedule, it is doubtful that any long-term, effective, educational change will occur. As a corollary, if I am a strong manager who can make an organization run very smoothly with timetables, clean bathrooms, coverage in the halls, but I have no idea of leadership and personal leadership traits, the instructional part of leadership may atrophy and the students will suffer.

Therefore, it is important to have a repertoire of knowledge of leadership in general, leadership traits of an individual, and effective management strategies. It is important to recognize that no one idea works all the time or in all situations. It is important to have a strong theoretical background, and it is equally important to have the reflective, self-examination skills to be able to change approaches and strategies of leadership and management when necessary.

Purpose of This Book . . .

This book is designed to be a handbook for administrators, particularly those new to the task, to have one resource for the many components that make up the job of school administrator. Each chapter is devoted to a topic that, if researched individually, has been described at length by hundreds of books and articles. This book is a handbook with the major topics in one volume.

This handbook provides an introduction or overview to the area and then suggests further resources for more in-depth study, if needed. For some chapters, readers may want to explore further. For others, the basic knowledge or review is all that is necessary. There are questions at the end of each chapter for personal reflection and for group study, so that this handbook may be used as a text for professional development among peers or as a personal journal.

Questions are provided, but the process used for each group discussion may be different, depending on the context of the group. There are some excellent resources on facilitating group discussion.

Elaine McEwan's book on *10 Traits* (2003) has a section in the back of the book on facilitating group discussion. Garmston and Wellman (1999) have many wonderful suggestions on facilitation of group process. It is unnecessary for me to repeat such good work already well outlined by others.

Within each of the topics, the theoretical ideas are integrated with management strategies. The two are interwoven so that the administrator does not have to waste time discovering how to manage a topic but can concentrate on the leadership aspects.

Summary

Therefore, because of the need for knowing about leadership theory, for knowing what personal leadership traits make an effective school leader, and for having management strategies, this book starts by exploring theories of leadership and leadership traits.

Next, the book discusses individual topics by providing an overview and then providing practical suggestions for management of the topic.

Finally, the book brings the discussion to the level of a reflective practitioner. Unless a person can take global theories, translate them to daily work topics, and incorporate them into personal behavior, leadership will not occur. The book begins at its most global perspective and becomes increasingly personal so that strategies and ideas become routinized. The reflective skill is emphasized also within each topic at the end of each chapter.

Some would say that management is a skill and leadership is an art. However, an effective principal, a leader, does both.

> As for the best leaders,
> the people do not notice their existence.
> The next best,
> the people honor and praise.
> The next, people fear
> and the next the people hate.
> When the best leader's work is done,
> the people say, we did it ourselves.
>
> —Lao-Tzu, 6th century B.C.

Personal Journal

How do I blend management needs with leadership skills?

What are my strengths as a manager? As a leader?

It is important to reflect on professional practices. When was the last time I read and reflected about leadership?

Group Discussion

1. How does an effective school leader decide how to approach the culture of a building? How does a leader decide what approach to take?

2. What are some situations where certain leadership theories may not work?

3. What should a leader do when something is not working?

PART II

Topical Issues

2

A Neat Desk Is
Not Necessarily
the Sign of a
Good Administrator

The first chapter of this book discussed theories of leadership and management. One of the most important management skills for an effective school leader is the ability to manage time well. Without effective time management skills, a leader is too fragmented, distracted, and overwhelmed to perform the leadership duties. Plus, there is a tendency to let the mundane get in the way of the glorious.

A common complaint heard in staff lounges, hallways, and boardrooms is that there is never enough time. It is my experience that the mantra of not enough time is an excuse, an excuse that creates inertia because who can argue with the fact that people are busy and lead busy lives.

One of the most important strategies for effective time management is to develop a healthy attitude toward time. What is important is HOW a person spends time. We all have the same amount of time and we all find time to do what we think is important. It's about the responsibility we own for how we CHOOSE to spend our time. As a corollary, after making those choices, it is not necessary to feel guilty about what was or was not accomplished. Using the excuse of not enough time sometimes lets people off the hook from not accomplishing what they desire.

It is ironic that if one does not choose actively how to spend time, time will pass by anyway. During that time a person will be doing something, so in effect, has made a choice.

It is important to recognize that a person does not have to be engaged in activities every second of the day. Everyone needs time to contemplate, reflect, and think. Everyone needs time to interact on a personal basis. What is important is for people to recognize that we each choose how to spend our time and we can choose to spend it in a manner that is productive, yet humane.

Beginning Strategies

• It is important to assess current practices. How do you spend your time? Keep a log for a week. How much time is spent in ways that are not helpful? How much time do you spend chatting? Do you plan for exercise? Where do you work best with the fewest distractions? Do you waste a lot of time doing errands because you do not plan the route or do you spread the errands out over many days instead of doing several in one day?

• Schedule things that matter and make those things happen. Schedule observations for the year into the calendar so they do not get left until the last minute. Plan time for professional socializing, such as being in the staff lunchroom to visit with teachers. Plan for time to be in classes to observe learning, which is always a way to recharge and remember why we are in the profession.

• Recognize that informal conversations such as in the lunchroom, hallways, and staff lounge are very productive. One gathers information and is sometimes able to put out fires before they erupt. For example, one day I was in the halls before school started. A staff member came up to me with the famous line, "Just to let you know . . ." which usually signals an item that is circulating among the staff but is most likely something the principal needs to know. This staff member shared that another teacher was going through a nasty divorce and was having a hard time getting through the days. I asked the staff member if it was okay that I "knew" this information and could approach the staff member or was this a secret. I was able to go to the staff member, and we were able to strategize some ways for her to get support.

These informal conversations are reminiscent of the business that is often conducted on a golf course by CEOs, or even superintendents. Although they appear casual, they are important to the function of McEwan's Culture Builder for the educational leader.

Annual Goals

- Collins' (2001) "Level 5 Leader" is a disciplined person who uses disciplined thought to demonstrate disciplined action (p. 127). Therefore, every good administrator sets annual goals so that energy and attention are focused. It is important to keep the goals simple, realistic, attainable, and few in number. Doug Reeves, author of *Holistic Accountability* (2002), believes that no one or no organization is able to work on more than six things at a time. I would suggest having no more than three.

If there are three major tasks to accomplish in a year, there is a lot of work involved. We all know that other issues arise on a daily basis that take time and energy. Therefore, it is unrealistic to think that a leader can accomplish all things at all times.

As Collins (2001) said, a good idea is not a good idea if it takes away from the mission of the organization. He goes so far as to suggest developing a "stop doing list" (p. 139). We are eager to create *to do* lists, but we forget to talk about what to *stop* doing. By having specific limited goals, we are able to do precisely that. We create a focus for budget expenditures, energy, and professional development. Three goals are enough. If another idea comes along, the leader can say, "No, we cannot tackle that this year. I'll put it in a tickler file for consideration for next year because it is a good idea. But this year our energy is focused on . . ."

- Goals, both personal and professional, need to be SMART—Specific, Measurable, Attainable, Realistic, and Tangible. An example of a personal goal could be to "Utilize the grade level teams to gather data and assess progress for reading scores at all grade levels." This is different from "Improve the reading scores for fourth grade."

It is specific to reading and can be measured by the work of the teams. It is attainable because a leader can devote time to the issue to make certain it happens. The goal is realistic, if this has been identified as a need. Improving reading is definitely tangible.

The same goal could be even more specific if it were used on a site plan by saying that the goal was to "Improve the fourth grade reading scores by 10% across all levels."

Involved in the goal for the administrator is to know about the management pieces of accountability, data-driven leadership, professional development, curriculum, and special education, to name a few. The leader will have to facilitate the interaction of the above pieces in order for the goal to happen.

Too often people write goals that are so lofty that they cannot be accomplished. People fear that they will be judged as not working hard enough if the goals are not grand. However, that becomes defeating. It is important to remember that smaller goals are steppingstones to larger accomplishments. Set a doable goal for this year and build on it next year.

- Site goals and personal goals should align with the priorities of the district. It is amazing the number of site plans that do not reflect the goals of the district. How, then, can the district be moving toward the same ends?

- After establishing goals, look at the yearly calendar and schedule meetings or reflection times to revisit the goals throughout the school year so that June, and the final performance meeting with the supervisor, is not a mad scramble.

- At the end of the year, summarize the accomplishments on the goals.

- While summarizing the year's accomplishments, pull out the tickler file to see if any of those good ideas that came up throughout the year could be incorporated and then establish goals for the following year. Too often administrators put off the formal writing of their goals until the day before, or the day of, the meeting with the supervisor. It is an efficient and productive use of time to do summary goals and next year's goals at one time. Besides, it makes sense.

Monthly Concerns

Schools are very cyclical and rhythmical. In planning, school leaders need to be conscious of these cycles, particularly in looking at implementation points. Most times we implement new initiatives, such as new curriculum adoptions, or new technology implementations, at the beginning of the school year. If that cannot happen, we often have to wait until the following year. Sometimes, however, we can begin a pilot at a semester break, but that is usually on a small scale. Schools spend a lot of time on starting and stopping. Business does not understand about these rhythms.

Elementary and secondary schools have differing rhythms. Some districts have conferences, for example, at different times for elementary and secondary schools. Some districts allow sites to make decisions about how to spend their conference time to reflect differing needs by different development levels.

Timing for professional development opportunities may be different depending on the level. It is important to consider the rhythms of a school and a district in looking at how time is best used. For example, elementary teachers want training on the Basic Reading Inventory to help identify reading levels of their first graders. It is important that this is done at the end of a school year so it can be incorporated at the start of the following year. Training for this in mid-December would be counterproductive.

Some monthly strategies are:

- Establish a calendar of what has to be done each month. Establish a file for each month in a file drawer, or better yet on the computer, about what must happen. For example, in high schools the registration guide comes out in December so all write-ups must be done in November. Therefore, in October the staff meeting must address the timeline. These deadlines can be put on a monthly calendar.

- Following are some other possible items for monthly files.

  1. September—start up, getting to know students

     Get ready for Open House

     Get ready for Curriculum nights

     Plan for Homecoming, if it's early

  2. October—

     Plan for Homecoming

     Progress reports and midquarters come out

     Conferences with parents. Students who do not excel in school often fall apart around the fifth week of school—when midterms come out—because it is apparent that they still are not successful in school. So be prepared to deal with student issues such as not turning in homework, poor attendance, lack of achievement, etc.

Many Individual Education Plans (IEPs) are due in October

Schedule the first observation of nontenured teachers

3. November—anticipation of the holidays

Closing out of first quarter

Report cards due

4. December—Making certain material is covered before winter break

Curriculum meetings scheduled before the end of the semester

Schedule more observations in the first two weeks of December

Review progress on personal goals. How am I doing?

5. January—End of second quarter and grades

Begin thinking and planning for next year

Schedule observations but avoid the last week of the quarter and the first week of the new quarter

6. February—Doldrums

Try to do observations of tenured teachers

Mid-quarter reports come out

7. March—testing

End of third quarter. Report cards or reports

Prepare for conferences

It may be spring break, if people have one

Plan for professional development or curriculum that must be developed over the summer break

Budgets due

8. April—testing

Schedule final observation of nontenured teachers

Staffing decisions are made

9. May—Need to finish up with curriculum review projects

Begin thinking about next year in earnest

10. June—Wrap-up

Some curriculum writing, some professional development to prepare for next year

Final goal setting for administrators

Write summary for personal goals and set next year's goals

11.   July and August—

Sort all electronic and paper files

Finish schedules and class assignments

Do annual rollover in the schedule to start the new year

Publish class assignments

Prepare opening principal's newsletter

• Budget cycles. Schools are inherently governed by annual budget cycles. Depending on how state allocations are made, school budgets must react accordingly. Often schools are making staffing decisions before state allocations have been finalized. Certain grant applications, such as for Title funds, must be done at certain times of the year. Budget projections must be in the business office by a certain month. Note these deadlines on the monthly planner so that they are not being completed at the last minute.

• On a monthly basis plan for professional development time in the building, either in staff meetings, professional development days, or after and before school activities. Block out some possible time. The dates can be changed but if not allotted for, too often this important activity is done on a piecemeal basis.

• Schedule all the standing meetings on the monthly planner at the beginning of the year. Principal meetings, administrative council meetings, PTA, parent conferences, curriculum nights, and so on are all meetings that can be put on the planner at the beginning of the year and, hopefully, avoid being "double-booked."

• Most principals work from 50 to 70 hours a week by the time they supervise activities. To stay healthy, administrators have to set a time limit on how much they are willing to devote to the job. An unhealthy administrator is of no value to the self or the organization. So plan time each month for personal needs, such as scheduling vacations, exercise time, and time doing things such as getting massages.

• Plan for personal professional development opportunities. Pick one or two outstanding conferences a year to get new ideas and broaden one's professional network. Block times on the monthly calendar because most national conferences are scheduled years in advance. For example, Association for Curriculum and Development (ASCD); National Staff Development Council (NSDC); and principal organizations. National Association of Secondary School Principals (NASSP), National Association of Elementary School Principals (NAESP), and National Middle School Association (NMSA) have Web sites where one can see where and when the conference is scheduled. Attending a national conference at least every two years is vital in order to stay current in all of the management and leadership pieces that make a professional learning community.

Daily Use of Time

To manage the year and month, an effective school leader begins by examining how to manage each day. Too often administrators let the day dictate the structure of the time, instead of the leader planning it out. It is important to know one's best time of day, tools that are helpful, and how to plan the day.

A caveat, of course, is to be prepared for the ever-present interruptions and to recognize that flexibility is important. Sometimes what we plan for is not what happens, in spite of our best intentions. Robert Burns' line from "To a Mouse" sums it up well. "The best-laid schemes o'mice an'men/Gang aft a-gley, [go oft awry]" (p. 27, Norton Anthology).

- One strategy is to come in an hour before most teachers arrive to take care of paperwork. Or some people prefer to stay an hour after all activities are done to do this work in the evening. One of the quietest hours is the second hour after teachers have gone home. Parents believe the school is closed and call less frequently. Drop-ins by teachers are less frequent.

I used to arrive an hour ahead of the teachers and before my secretary. However, there are some early-bird teachers as well, who discover that you are available and will come and chat, or conduct business.

Some administrators schedule a certain time every week and then close their door. Because my door was always open, when it was closed was a signal that teachers and students quickly learned meant that I was unavailable.

The exact strategy is not important. What is important is to find a time that works for you. Then make use of that time so it is not whittled away. An effective leader will use concentrated, undistracted time either in an office at home or in the building on the weekends to draft memos, write up evaluations, or do other paperwork. It is more efficient to find one hour of uninterrupted quiet space and accomplish several tasks, than it is to try to do them when the telephone rings and people stop in. One hour of concentration can often accomplish what cannot be done in three hours with interruptions. Find what and where works best for you.

• Plan at least one time to be visible in the halls during passing, lunchtime, and after school each day.

• Schedule visits to classrooms at least three times a week. Let the secretary block that time on the daily calendar so that time does not slip by and all of the observations get clustered at crunch time late in the school year. Teachers respect the fact that an administrator cares to be in classrooms early in the year and often. Even if the times are scheduled on the calendar, a crisis often usurps them. But if they are not scheduled in, they certainly will not happen.

A caveat about working at home or in school on weekends. Be careful about devoting work time to work and home time to home. No one ever put on their tombstone that they wish they had spent more time at work. However, sometimes people wish they had spent more time with their families. The job will never be DONE, but it is done ENOUGH.

Managing the Mail

We now get mail in four ways: "snail mail" or regular mail, voice mail solicitations, e-mail, and fax. It is important to manage all of this so it does not take too much time. Some of it is important, and some is "junk."

• One way to deal with the snail mail that comes to the office is to have the secretary sort it into three categories: important—mail that needs to be read today; this week mail—what needs to be dealt with this week; and whenever-mail—the stuff one can take home and sort. Most of whenever-mail will be recyclable.

• Develop a system that works for dealing with the mail. Take time either before the day begins to sort through mail or do it at the end of the day. This is also something that can be done if there are a few minutes between meetings. However, the today mail often needs some type of interaction quickly.

- Take enough time so that when going through the mail, you handle each item only once. Read it, decide what must be done, and then deal with it accordingly, by filing it, forwarding it to the appropriate party, or tossing it.

- Train the secretary as to which flyers, catalogs, and solicitations are unnecessary for you to see. Have her recycle them as she goes through them. There is no need to touch every piece of mail that is addressed to you.

- Unsolicited e-mails are another waste of time. Reputable organizations will have an "unsubscribe" on the bottom of the e-mail. Do that. Send it back, usually with unsubscribe in the subject line. Take yourself off as many lists as possible. However, there are some disreputable e-mails, such as those from Africa, China, and Uzbekistan that do not allow for unsubscribing. Learn their format and delete without opening, because the more you open them, the more you will receive.

- There are advertisements and solicitations that come via e-mail from some mysterious mailing lists. If possible, work with the technology department to block as many as possible, particularly the pop-ups on the Internet. The more one opens those unsolicited e-mails, the more you will get because of the "cookies" that are sent.

- We now get solicitations through faxes as well. Work with the secretary to just toss them away. Again, it is not necessary for you to handle each piece of mail that comes your way.

Technology, Organizational Tools, and Strategies

1. E-mail, etc. We have more tools for communication than ever before and we have more demands to communicate in different formats than ever before.

E-mails are an efficient use of time, if used correctly. They can be a way to answer questions from parents or staff quickly and avoid the need for a face-to-face meeting, which almost always takes longer. E-mail is also a way to deliver the same message to several people at one time by addressing a response or notification to many people at once. It is a handy way to find the best time for a meeting so that time is not wasted on the telephone trying to schedule many busy people.

But a person does need to develop a system to deal with the e-mails. One option is to open e-mails and try to take care of those before school starts. Some e-mails need extra work. It will be important to try to take care of those as quickly and efficiently as possible. As soon as the e-mail has been answered or dealt with, either file it in a file folder, or delete it.

Too many e-mails in the inbox are confusing and take too much time to scroll through each day. Set up your e-mail box so that the most current is first, which also saves time spent scrolling through lists.

If important e-mails must be kept, set up an electronic folder and file it, or, if necessary, print it out and file it in hard copy. Then delete the e-mail from the inbox. One administrator had over 200 e-mails in her inbox and could not sort through important, current, spam, etc. Keep no more than 50 in the inbox at any one time to avoid wasting time scrolling through them. Open e-mail before school, at lunch, and right after school. There is an unwritten etiquette that senders expect a response within 24 hours with e-mail. If you need time to gather more information, send a response with that message. Then get back to the sender as soon as possible.

Language used in e-mail must be written carefully so that people do not misinterpret the message. E-mail, unlike telephone or face-to-face, does not have the blessing of intonation of voice, body language, or facial expression. It is important to craft messages carefully so that messages are not misunderstood. If there is a concern about how the e-mail "sounds," have someone else read it before pushing the Send button.

In like fashion, it is sometimes tempting to draft hurried responses to received e-mails that appear rude, impertinent, or just plain rotten. It is unwise to fire off an immediate response. Wait a few hours, draft a response, and even ask someone else to read it. Or, read it aloud to see if it sounds harsh. Try to pick up any sarcastic or harsh words. Read it as though you were the receiver, not the sender, and see how you would respond.

2. Voice mail messages. It is good practice to pick up voice mail messages at least three times a day—in the morning, at lunch, and at the end of the day. Many people pick up the message as soon as they see a light blinking. Keep a telephone log to write down messages. It is helpful to keep a telephone log with date, time of call, caller, message, and date of response. Date the log and check it off or highlight it with a magic marker when you have responded.

There is an unwritten etiquette that telephone messages will also be answered within 24 hours. If you are going to be out of the building for a day or more and are not going to pick up messages, put that message on your machine so that people are not expecting to hear from you right away.

3. Fax. Some business correspondence can be taken care of by fax. Registrations for conferences, registrations for professional development, book orders, etc. are only a few. Send the fax and then keep a hard copy to document the transaction. If you receive a message that needs a faxed reply, do it and then get the item off your desk.

For any correspondence, be it email, telephone, fax, or snail mail, try to handle items only once. Answer the question, forward the message, make the appointment, alert other parties—do whatever it takes to complete the action to get it off the desk and out of mind.

4. Palm pilot. Some administrators still trust the paper planners more than the electronic ones. For some, it is almost a badge of courage to avoid Palms. However, once a person gets familiar with all the possibilities, Palm Pilots can be an asset. They may be used as a date book, camera, database, portable laptop, and now some are cell phones. A planner cannot do all of that.

One of the most time-efficient capabilities of a Palm is in the calendar option. It is particularly helpful to have the ability to sync with your secretary so both can see the calendar and make additions. The calendar can be viewed on the computer by day, month, or year. It can automatically schedule repeated meetings, such as principal meetings so that they only have to be entered once, unlike a paper planner where each item is entered individually. This does save time.

One hint learned by accident is that I enter items in lower case letters; my secretary enters hers in upper case. Then I can see who put the item on my calendar if I need more information about the purpose and/or whereabouts of the meeting.

Another feature of the Palm is Documents-to-Go where individuals may generate word documents or other documents, which can be uploaded to the desktop computer for more work or for printing. A collapsible keyboard that attaches to the Palm quickly converts it to a very portable laptop computer that can be used to take notes in a car, conference, or meeting without using as much room in the briefcase or on the table when it is being used as a laptop.

Palms also have picture-taking capabilities in some models, which are helpful for administrators as they monitor hallways or need to take pictures of events, such as bathroom graffiti. Some Palms have the student yearbook downloaded so that the principal can identify an unknown student very quickly.

Palms can be used for teacher evaluation. The teacher evaluation form can be entered on the Palm so that the administrator can spend more time actually observing, rather than writing. The administrator is able to observe more closely and just make notations on the Palm. In addition, there are counting tools that can be used with the joystick if the administrator is observing for the number of times a teacher asks a probing question, calls on girls versus boys, etc. Then, when the administrator gets back to the office, the data is on the Palm and can be used in discussing the observation with the teacher.

A principal can also have other documents such as the staff directory downloaded to the Palm. Telephone numbers would be readily available. Not having the directory on paper also saves the time and cost of printing. In addition, the information can be kept current more easily without waiting for the annual update.

5. Calendar tools. There are calendar tools both in Palm Pilots and in email systems that can be used to share appointments. Some email systems ask if the appointment is to be shared with others. By saying yes, the appointment is scheduled very easily with multiple parties.

There are even specific calendars that can be shared with a particular user group. For example, we have set one up for professional development activities. There are some days when there are not enough substitutes and our sub caller has no way to know when these heavy use dates are coming. So we set up a calendar so that anyone who plans professional development activities can enter the dates, number of subs, level (elementary or secondary), and activity. The sub callers, building secretaries, curriculum and professional development people, and principals all have access so they can enter or see which days have heavy use and can either avoid those days or start planning for subs. The calendar can be viewed by day, month, or year. It is very helpful.

In Palm software, there is a calendar feature as well. It is helpful to have the software loaded onto the secretary's machine. It is important to sync (synchronize) with the secretary's on a daily basis so that both parties know what is happening. Both parties can also schedule meetings without having to coordinate the effort verbally.

6. Shared folders or Intranet. There is the capability to have shared folders on the computer restricted to a set of users. There can be shared folders for elementary principals, secondary principals, cabinet, all administrators, and so on. Any member of that group can enter data. This is particularly helpful for groups who meet on a regular basis for establishing agendas. Any member of the group can enter an item on the agenda or establish a folder that all members can see.

Such a practice builds shared responsibility without making any one person responsible for agendas or content.

There is also the capability to have an Intranet on the district network where certain members have user rights. The staff may have an Intranet guarded by a password so they can access all district forms, copies of the contract, district notices, staff handbooks, and so on. Information that district members need can be stored electronically and updated easily in this fashion. By publishing such data electronically, the need for paper handbooks is erased and, once again, paper and printing costs are saved.

7. Use of laptops. As wireless Internets become more common, the use of laptops to take notes, access email, access the Internet and integrate technology into the classroom will become more and more common. As laptops become lighter and cheaper, the ability to use technology will expand in ways we have not even begun to realize.

8. Databases and spreadsheets. Databases and spreadsheets are helpful and important tools to learn. Most people relegate the use of these tools to their clerical support staff, but occasionally the leader is in a situation with a need to work with data. There are introductory classes, which are short, or there are books, particularly in the "Dummy" series, that are helpful tools. In our era of accountability, collecting and managing data, asking the right questions, and trying to discover causality, it is more than helpful for leaders to be able to use such electronic tools easily.

9. PowerPoint. Contemporary audiences expect technological presentations, making it crucial for leaders to know how to put together a PowerPoint presentation. There are classes, or again, there is *Power-Point for Dummies* by IDG Books, which is an excellent resource. PowerPoint allows for a more dramatic and visually pleasing presentation because diagrams, photos, graphs, and other visual aids can be imported to establish a presentation in a way that overheads cannot. However, some users try to use PowerPoint as though it were an electronic overhead. It is not!!!

It is important to understand some important principles:

- Use the 6-by-6 rule—*No more than six lines per slide and no more than six words in each line.* I cannot emphasize this enough. Too often presenters try to include every word from their notes onto a slide and the slides are too cluttered and unreadable, particularly if people have to read from a computer screen. The *Powerpoint for Dummies* book says to use only five lines, but adults have a hard time sticking to that.

- Each slide is meant to be a mnemonic guide for presentation; it is not to be a written report. Therefore, do not include everything on the slide that is in the written document. If the presenter needs to present graphs or charts, do that in hard copy so that they are readable. The presenter also needs to understand that some graphs that use colors or different types of lines—dashes, solid, and so on—do not show up clearly on computer screens or when the presentation is broadcast on local TV stations.

- Use the slide as a visual reminder. Do not read the information to the audience. Just as speech teachers teach their students not to read the speech word for word, do not read the slide. Elaborate only.

- Be careful in using the gimmicky transition tools. Use the transitions rarely where words fly in from the sides, or bottom, or top. If the transition is used to highlight or emphasize one particular point, it may be a helpful tool. If used too often, it becomes a trite distraction. Do not mix transitions in the same slide because that becomes too distracting. Avoid the sounds—like the typewriter or the whoosh—because the sounds trivialize the content of the presentation.

- If the presentation is to be broadcast on cable television, for example, such as a presentation for the school board, make sure any charts or graphs have a font size that is large enough for people to see. If the presentation when printed on hard copy has graphs that cannot be seen, then do not use them on a PowerPoint slide. Find a different way of making the information visual. A graph that is not readable is worse than no graph at all.

- Do not put a chart into a PowerPoint just because you can; only do it if it is legible and meaningful. If not, find another way to share the information.

- Rehearse the presentation before the actual time. There is nothing more embarrassing than to have preventable mistakes.

- Time the presentation so that it is no more than ten minutes. Then leave five to ten minutes for questions. If it is longer than that, the audience will begin to lose focus.

- Use font size of 24 and do not mix more than two font styles on a slide. One style could be for heading and another for sub points. Other than that, too many font styles make the presentation look sloppy and unprofessional.

- Contrary to Mrs. Jones, your high school English teacher, do NOT use complete sentences on the slides; use sound bytes. The presenter will make the sentences complete. Do not clutter the slide.

- Go to the site of the presentation and make sure all the equipment works ahead of the presentation. Bring your own laptop and projector if that makes it easier.

Do not blame technology for not working if it is you, as presenter, who has not prepared adequately.

- Remember—a PowerPoint presentation is not the same as a written report. It is a different tool so use it accordingly.

10. Cell phones. The discussion of technology would definitely not be complete without a discussion of cell phones. Cell phones are a time saver and time drainer, depending on how one uses them. If the nature of the job is that people need to be able to get in touch at all times, cell phones are invaluable. Certainly, they are helpful in adding to flexibility and in having emergency access.

However, it is important to use them wisely. One can set up times to connect with secretaries so that a person does not receive a call during a meeting. The rude interruption by cell phones is becoming one of the curses of the 21st century. So turn it off when it is not necessary.

It is not necessary to give out the cell phone number to everyone. Give out the desk phone, call in for messages, and then return calls when it is appropriate.

Safety would suggest that one should not make calls while driving. Some districts have policies saying employees cannot conduct district business on cell phones while driving during work time. If it is necessary to make a call while in a car, pull over and make the call in the parking lot before getting on the road.

Cell phones are also becoming more sophisticated with the addition of cameras, emails, and I-Messaging. It is important to use the tool; do not let the tool dictate to you.

Summer Organizational Strategies

1. Go through all files both electronic and paper over the summer. Too often we leave electronic messages on the desktop computer, but most technology directors will ask people to clean out their files because saved messages require server space. The more we keep, the more server space is needed which adds to the technology budget.

Throw away any paper or electronic files that have not been used in two years unless they have a historical bearing on future decisions. For example, there is a paper file on boundary decisions. The district is about to look at this issue again so save the pertinent charts and discussions. If, however, there is a file on a task force that was looking at a data drill-down system that has been purchased, it is probably safe to recycle the paper or delete the electronic file.

2. Educators are packrats. We have a tendency to keep everything because we may need it again. However, information changes so quickly that the ability to reuse it is less than it has been in the past because of the speed of change and the accessibility of information online. If information has not been used in the past two years and it is not required by law to retain, toss it or delete it. (It actually feels good to do this.)

Other Strategies

1. Handle it once. Try to handle mail, whether paper or electronic, only once. This is a terrific strategy to keep a leader from wasting time.

Try to do the same with minutes from a meeting. Right after a meeting, if there are minutes to prepare, or items to take care of, do it right away and finish with the piece of paper in hand and put it away. Do not just lay it on the desk to be dealt with later.

Try to handle other issues, whether curriculum, professional development, or special education, in the same manner. When an item crosses your desk, try to deal with it. Procrastination only leads to frustration.

Delegation is an important tool in handling items once. If someone is asking for information, give it to the appropriate person. If you have to get a person for a committee, get the member and turn over the task of that committee to the new member. Use your staff to take care of the clerical details as much as possible.

2. Friday afternoons. Friday afternoons after lunch are a good time to take care of weekly items that have been hanging. It is a good feeling to leave for the weekend by being well prepared for Monday and the upcoming week. Clearing away items on Friday also allows the leader to go home and rest and leave work both mentally and physically.

3. Delegate. Neal Nickerson, professor in Educational Policy and Administration at the University of Minnesota, Minneapolis, has words of advice for administrators. "Delegate—or die." Words to live by.

Give tasks to the appropriate person. It is not necessary for the leader to chair every committee, oversee every effort, or answer every letter. However, when the leader delegates, then one must also let go of the results, which is almost counterintuitive to some because of personal high standards.

The job may not be completed the same way the administrator would do it. Sometimes the task is not done as well as expected; but sometimes it is even better. Whichever is the case, remember that by not having to do certain tasks, you, as leader, were more able to do others. Plus, a leader is building skills in other people by delegating tasks to them. The titular school leader is not the only person who can complete leadership tasks. So delegate, and then let go.

When someone else takes over a task, be sure to acknowledge the work. Do so genuinely and honestly, but a simple thank you goes a long way to create a culture of appreciation and camaraderie.

4. Have one space that is clear. Have one space in the desk area or on the table, if there is one in the office, that is always kept clear and clean. It is psychologically appealing. Work with the secretary so that items are kept away from that area. Too much clutter keeps a person unfocused because one has a tendency to go from one pile to another without ever completing a task.

5. Retain flexibility. Interruptions are our business. Even with the best of intentions of completing a project at one sitting, or handling mail in one sitting, it may not happen. The job is a people-related job and people have needs. If something comes up, deal with it and then go back to the task. Getting frustrated is wasted energy!

How Do These Time-Management Strategies Facilitate Leadership and Leaders?

Time management is an integral part of leadership. Such strategies are not important in isolation, only in how they facilitate and allow leadership to blossom. It does not matter if someone is seen as efficient, if that efficiency does not lead to leadership.

Summary

A neat desk is not necessarily the sign of a good administrator. Our society places value on having a neat desk. The old sign "A neat desk is the sign of a cluttered mind" resonates because with all the pressures, distractions, and people involved with an administrator, it is impossible to have a desktop that is completely clean. In fact, a busy person has a busy workspace. Hopefully, some of the strategies above will help maintain a certain order so that the leader can focus on the truly important issues at hand.

Macbeth said it best:

"To-morrow, and to-morrow, and to-morrow,

Creeps in this petty pace from day to day

To the last syllable of recorded time." (Act V, Scene V, p. 1004)

Personal Journal

1. What strategies can I incorporate to make better use of my time?

2. What is one of the most common ways that I fritter away time?

3. How can I use technology to simplify my life?

Group Discussion

1. How can we use day-to-day management to facilitate leadership?

2. What are ways that I allow management to get in the way of leadership? Do I spend too much time doing tasks that could be delegated to support persons?

3

People Are
Our Business

In addition to managing time, a leader has to manage staff. One of the important tasks of a school leader is to facilitate, particularly with staff, the "deep connection" as defined by Rachel Kessler, author of *The Soul of Education: Helping Students Find Connection, Compassion and Character at School* (2000). Some of the deep connection is created because a leader does a good job of managing various aspects of staff interaction.

Hiring the Best Teachers

One of the most important tasks to create a professional learning environment and community, a strategy that combines leadership and management, is to hire the best teachers. Whitaker in his book *What Great Principals Do Differently* (2003) stated, "A principal's single most precious commodity is an opening in the teaching staff. The quickest way to improve your school is to hire great teachers at every opportunity" (p. 43).

By hiring the best teachers, the principal shapes the academic accomplishment of the students and school culture. "Experience is not the best teacher. The best teacher is the best teacher" (Whitaker, 2003, p. 46). His comment is reminiscent of Jim Collins' belief in *Good to Great* (2001) that it is important to have the right people on the bus, and in the right seats, and the wrong people off the bus (p. 39). Collins believes that people are not the most important asset; the *right* people are the most important asset.

Therefore, in hiring, in addition to training and experience, a leader must be aware of those teachers that demonstrate inner motivation and commitment. Look for those who have energy and passion for what they do.

The teacher with the most experience may not be the best teacher. The highest grade point average may not signal the best teacher. A good administrator can help facilitate professional development or training, but the candidate needs to have passion, enthusiasm, spirit of caring, and love of the profession all of which are highly contagious and effective. An administrator has the sheer joy of facilitating their growth, helping smooth their way, and let them work their miracles. Strong teacher-leaders rarely send students to the office. They rarely contribute to the negativism of teacher lounges. Great teachers do great things.

Hiring the best people allows the leader to lead, not manage. According to Collins (2001) having the right people decreases the need for "stultifying bureaucracy" because "bureaucratic cultures arise to compensate for incompetence and lack of discipline" (p. 142). A strong teacher-leader does not need more management but more facilitation. Helping them discover new professional development opportunities, ways to integrate technology, or design differentiated lessons are ways to manage the system and not the people. So hire good people, help smooth their way, and help support their journey.

Support and Conflict

Any time two people are together, there is a possibility of support and of conflict. Effective leaders must be able to manage both.

Support

One of the most important things a school leader does is support, encourage, and lead. In his book *What Great Principals Do Differently* (2003) Todd Whitaker describes what this support looks like:

- "It's people, not programs" (Whitaker, p. 8). There is no magic bullet curricula or program. It takes great teachers to make great changes. So great administrators surround themselves with great people. It is Collins' (2001) getting the right people on the bus—and in the right seats on that bus. Then the leader supports the efforts of those people.

- High expectations matter (Whitaker, 2003, p. 17). Great schools have teachers who expect a lot from themselves. Those effective schools have principals who support those teachers as they work to achieve their goals.

- "Treat Everyone With Respect, Every Day, All the Time" (p. 21). The principal sets the tone for the building. If the administrator operates from respect, then it is expected that teachers treat students With respect and that parents are respected. This attitude permeates the culture so that everyone from receptionists to food service employees creates a respectful, supportive community.

- "Make it cool to Care" (p. 89). A school leader cares about the people in the building and district, from the bus drivers to the parents. It is important to show that in small ways—by attending weddings, sending birthday cards, to saying "thank you" for a job well done.

- Build relationships and eliminate the sense of fear that comes from the hierarchy. Kessler (2002) quotes an assistant superintendent who said, "It's just so hard to make changes there when the system runs on hierarchy. How can we build that trust when people are so afraid to reveal themselves in a climate of fear?" (p. 24). To counteract the fear, it is important to build meaningful connections within all levels of the organization.

Supporting staff involves "helping people change themselves and their thinking," according to Michele Hancock with Barbara Lamendola in their recent article, "A Leadership Journey" (2005, p. 77). Sometimes leaders have to deal with "confused, stressed-out, cynical employees who wanted to do better but did not believe in their own potential or in the potential of their students . . ." (p. 77). The task of the leader becomes "to really listen to people, acknowledging their feelings without judgment. Gradually, we began to analyze and challenge our beliefs about student learning" (p. 77).

Kessler (2002) recognized the paradox inherent in creating supportive leadership. "Perhaps one of the most challenging paradox[es] a leader must hold today is the tension between standards and soul. . . . When soul and standards are honored and school leaders ride the paradox, an environment for learning is created that is strong enough to hold all the tensions, trends and turmoil of American life" (p. 26).

Strategies for Showing Support

1. Listening. The key factor in being supportive is to listen. There are two parts of listening. One, is to take the TIME to be with people, to know how they are, and what is happening in their classrooms.

Two is to listen for the REAL message. Administrators cannot know the REAL message unless they have a relationship and care about the individual.

Being a good listener means hearing the underlying message that may be hidden in the spoken words. For example, a teacher comes to discuss how "some" teachers are not doing their job (e.g., standing in the hall between classes). It may be that the real issue is that the next-door neighbor, who is not very likeable, is not doing supervision. The teacher wants the administrator to reprimand this person because it is not "fair" that some people do what is expected and others do not.

To get at real issues, the administrator must understand the culture of the organization, the personalities involved, and make decisions about the real issues. Therefore, the administrator must decide what action to take, if any. The action taken may be different than that requested by the message-giver because the administrator has to decide the real issue (Sigford, 1995, p. 76).

It is all about relationships.

2. Be visible. Greet the staff by the mailboxes in the morning. Notice new glasses or changes in hairstyle. Be in the halls with students. Be at events such as curriculum nights, athletic events, and concerts. Let staff know that you are available when they are having special events in the classroom to watch learning in progress.

3. Be friendly. A pleasant demeanor and smile go a long way to creating a culture where people feel valued.

4. Be accessible. An open door policy is important to create an atmosphere of support. If the leader is truly a good listener, staff will often use that person as a sounding board for professional and personal issues. Staff will share when they are going through divorce, when a parent is ill, or when a child is having a hard time. By listening, the leader helps build an intricate spider web of connection among staff members. Although spider webs appear fragile, in nature they are strong and very complex.

5. Care. There are many ways to show caring for others. One simple, obvious strategy is to send cards—birthday, sympathy, get well, just thinking of you.

Have a stash of cards in the office so that they are readily available. Cards are less likely to be sent if they are not readily available.

6. Schedule time on the personal planner to visit classrooms apart from teacher evaluations For many administrators this is personally recharging because one is reminded of why one went into this business—to see learning and to see kids be excited. For the staff, it builds a sense that the administrator really cares about what happens in the classroom.

Also, schedule time to go visit the food service and custodians in their offices to chat with them. They are an important part of the organization, and it is important that they feel valued as well. Besides, an administrator can learn a lot about the building and its culture by visiting employees in their workspace.

7. Use staff meetings as a combination of news, professional development, and acknowledgments. Staff meetings are a wonderful opportunity to build the web of connections within a staff. It sets a wonderful tone if the leader begins a staff meeting by recognizing something wonderful that has happened in the past month—Ms. So-and-So's students were recognized in the newspaper, Mr. So-and-So published an article, etc.

Feature a department or grade level each month so they can talk about a success that happened. Such information has two effects. One, people are able to acknowledge the good things that happen on a daily basis. Two, it breaks down barriers among grade levels and departments because teachers learn what their peers are doing in the classrooms.

Have teacher-leaders on the staff teach at a staff meeting. Ms. Wong is very knowledgeable about strategies to teach vocabulary. Have her demonstrate a lesson.

Mr. Wykovsky uses PDAs in a science experiment in a rich experience for students. Have him show the staff, or better yet, have a student demonstrate.

It is not necessary to use staff meetings as a bulletin board. Put announcements on an electronic staff Intranet and use the staff meetings for more adult items—sharing professional accomplishments and professional development.

Conflict

In like fashion, James McGregor Burns in his Pulitzer Prize–winning book, *Leadership* (1978), says that leaders "must settle for far less than universal affection. . . . They must accept conflict. They must be willing and able to be unloved."

Paradoxically, anytime two or more people can provide support, the opposite is also true; there is a possibility of conflict. It is difficult for educators to deal with conflict in an open, daily fashion. Educators will express their opposing views in teachers' lounges, in parking lots, or in conversations with close friends but hesitate to do so openly in a larger meeting.

A healthy organization is able to deal with conflict as it arises in a manner that treats people respectfully. It is the task of a leader to create an atmosphere where conflict is seen as healthy and is dealt with in an open, timely fashion.

Conflict can be systemic or personal. In addition, there are different levels of conflict. (There is more in-depth discussion of the levels of conflict in *Who Said School Administration Would Be Fun?* (2005) by Sigford).

Level One Conflict

Level one conflict contains those issues that can be dealt with relatively quickly. For level one conflict, there is a right and wrong. Issues can be resolved by appealing to policy, laws, or commonly held values. For example, it is wrong for someone to hit another person. Dealing with level one conflict can be accomplished by enforcing rules and applying logical consequences. Mediation, discussions, or simply telling someone to stop the behavior are strategies.

Level Two Conflict

Level two conflict is more involved. There is a difference of opinion or values that are not clear-cut and there is some responsibility on the part of each party. The perennial "he said, she said" type of arguments would fit this category.

If some of the level two conflicts are ignored, the disharmony may fester and come out in other ways. It is the task of an administrator to bring such issues to light. The leader may have to act as mediator or bring in another third party to help resolve the issue. Too often we ignore these conflicts, knowing that the urgency will go away. However, a skilled administrator will understand that the conflict does not really go away.

For example, two teachers had to share a workspace. One was neat and the other was just the opposite. Their disagreements were commonly known in the staff lounge. The administrator had to mediate between the two and draw up a contract about behavior. The issue resurfaced later in the year and the administrator had to go back to the contract and talk about the agreement. This conflict takes time to resolve.

Peer mediation strategies are helpful in this type of conflict. It is important to hear all sides and then listen for the real issue. Strategies from Fisher, Ury, and Patton's *Getting to Yes* (1991) are beneficial.

Level Three Conflict

Level three conflicts may not be able to be solved. It may be a dilemma, as opposed to a problem. Cuban's *How Can I Fix It?* (2001) describes the difference between a problem and a dilemma. A problem is an issue that has a solution. For example, students need more room for taking standardized tests so testing needs to be delivered in the gym, instead of in classrooms.

However, dilemmas must be managed. There is no one solution. For example, there is never enough time for professional development. Budget cuts have created even more cuts in available time. Therefore, leaders must find other avenues to deliver professional development—use a second staff meeting a month, pay teachers to come before or after school, and so on. There is no one answer and no one lasting solution.

Because dilemmas are rich in complexity, there may not be a permanent solution. In education, we too often treat dilemmas as problems and try to resolve them with simplistic solutions. We then end up revisiting the issue several times, frustrated that it has not been solved. However, it is important to change mindsets and recognize that level three conflicts will only be managed by a variety of methods.

Lower level conflicts can be solved. However, most of what happens in schools is level two or three conflicts, which are more time-consuming and stressful (Sigford, 1995, pp. 116–118).

Strategies for Dealing With Conflict

Describe the elephant in the middle of the living room. Too often we allow the hidden conflict to go unrecognized. If there are hidden issues, bring them out in the open. This may cause discomfort, but that is healthy. After watching elephants in the wild in Africa, this author recognizes that those large noble beings can cause damage, but mostly they glide silently and seemingly effortlessly through the grass. However, do not let this big critter glide.

Learn mediation skills. For personal conflict there are some excellent resources. William Ury's *Getting Past No* (1991) and Fisher et al.'s *Getting to Yes* (1991) are excellent sources of strategies for dealing with conflict. Todd Whitaker's book *Dealing With Difficult Teachers* (1999) and Elaine I. McEwan's *How to Deal With Parents Who Are Angry, Troubled, Afraid, or Just Plain Crazy* (1998) are all resources for further in-depth study. There are suggestions in my earlier book, *Who Said School Administration Would Be Fun? (2005).*

Conflict is a process, not an end. It is important to realize that conflict is a process, begging for attention. Therefore, it is important to recognize that it must be acknowledged as process. In education, we have a tendency to want closure so that we can move on to other tasks. However, we must learn to be comfortable with process and lack of finality. That is not easy for people who are so task oriented.

Conflict has stages: presentation of the issues, defining the issues, deriving solutions, and working on them. A conflict may not be resolved with one intervention but may have to be revisited. A leader must learn to be content with the process of conflict as a work in progress.

• **Give up the idea of a "quick-fix."** Because conflict is a process and it took time to appear, it will also take time to resolve, which is why a person must work "through" conflict. That's why therapists make money because people need time to understand and resolve issues. For example, the sixth-grade teachers of the middle school who teach science feel that other science teachers do not value what happens in the sixth-grade classroom. It will take time to articulate the curriculum, establish coordination with state standards, and have discussions with both the fifth-grade and seventh-grade staff to articulate across grade levels. Such a process takes time and work.

• **Remember that you, as administrator, are a facilitator. Do not personalize the conflict.** Understand that it is not about you. It is about the issue. Facilitate the resolution but do not personalize it. Absorbing all conflict that comes to an administrator's door will quickly lead to exhaustion and burnout.

• **Whose monkey is it?** Staff members look to the leader to listen and resolve conflict. Too often staff members want the administrator to be the "mother superior" and answer all questions, resolve all conflicts, and absolve them of their adult responsibility. For example, teachers come and talk about the issue in a department. They expect the principal to "fix" it. However, for administrators to stay healthy and not absorb all the ills of a building, it is important to listen to the issues and help other adults come up with solutions.

Staff come to "get the monkey off their back." They will try to give it to you. However, passing the "monkey" off to others absolves adults from taking the responsibility for their actions. After someone presents an issue to process, think quietly, "Whose monkey is this?" If it is a problem that should be dealt with by an administrator, then do so. However, and this is more often the case, staff come hoping to get themselves off the hook. Don't do it. Let them have their own monkey.

For example, a staff member comes forward with a "just for your information" and lets the principal know that a person who also teaches the tenth-grade social studies curriculum is not following the essential questions as outlined by the review process. It is important for the administrator to help the person discuss how to deal with the issue. This is an issue that can be dealt with first by the department. It is important for all tenth-grade teachers to get together and talk about what is expected. A department chair can facilitate this discussion. If it cannot be resolved at this level, then the administrator must step in and enforce the district expectations. It is healthy to solve it at the lowest level possible before the administrator has to step in.

Helping adults solve their own problems is healthy because when they own their issues and solve them, the issues are more likely to stay solved. Help by giving them verbal tools to use. Help them brainstorm as to the real issue. Ask questions so they can shape possible ways to address the issue. Help them solve it inductively because that is the way to build those skills in people and develop a healthier learning institution.

• **Don't give power to negative people.** Todd Whitaker (1999) wrote "we give too much power to these difficult people [i.e., negative teachers]" (p. 19). Too often we make decisions based on our desires to keep things calm or to not irritate these people, so that we forget to build on the positive forces.

In Chapter 10 of this book on effective meeting strategies, there is a tool called a Force Field analysis. When looking at ideas there are positive forces leading toward and negatives forces leading away. With negative people, too often we spend too much time trying to counteract the negative forces instead of spending more constructive time in building up the positive, which will then extinguish the negative forces.

Firefighters demonstrate this concept forcefully. To extinguish a fire, firefighters try to squelch the fire by using water or other flame-retardants. But they also know the importance of removing things that burn. In forest fires, firefighters often create firebreaks where they clear all things that burn. The fire literally dies from lack of fuel.

With negative people, take away their fuel. Put them on committees where they have to help to come up with a solution. Take away their leadership roles on negative committees. Better yet, surround them with positive people who are willing to put students first and almost "shame" the negative people into going along.

Bring their issues into the open. Negative leaders often operate from an informal, almost secretive power base. Keep the positive information going to the positive leaders so the negative leaders do not have an opportunity to sway opinion.

Remember, negative people have spent their lives being negative, and you cannot change that. For whatever reason, they derive energy from this negativity—that is "their monkey, not yours." Do not own it.

Also realize that you will not change them. They have spent a lot of time and practice in developing their coping strategies. But you can ameliorate their influence. Ultimately, if their negativity is harmful to students, you will need to conduct performance evaluations and call them on their behavior by establishing goals. If severe enough, you may need to work with the human resources department to work toward removal.

Labor Negotiations

Working in a school or district during the time of labor negotiations, particularly contentious negotiations, is the epitome of dealing with support and conflict. These times can be summed up with Charles Dickens's "it [is] the best of times, it [is] the worst of times, it [is] the age of wisdom, it [is] the age of foolishness" as stated in *A Tale Two Cities*. If negotiations go well, then staff members put the issue behind them and concentrate on the classroom.

If, however, there is "work to rule" or the threat of a strike, an administrator is in a fragile position, caught between supporting the staff and supporting the district. Even if the negotiations are moving forward without the threat of work to rule or strike, the time is automatically tense and conflictual.

Many districts are trying to do "interest-based bargaining" instead of the adversarial procedures that are commonly used. Negotiations are automatically polarized.

Even in the interest-based process, there is a sense among the staff that pits administrators and teachers against one another as though they have competing interests. A building principal is truly a "middle person." It is important to remain as neutral as possible.

In case of a strike, some principals, in order to continue the important relationships, have even brought food to picket lines. It is difficult to walk this tightrope of support with both teachers and district. It is important to keep language neutral and not discuss the process with anyone.

- Do not gossip or carry tales. Use the old *Dragnet* line by Jack Webb, "Just the facts, ma'am." Be true to yourself, but you, as an administrator, are part of the district. Your job is to administer. But you also must continue to have a relationship with your teachers in order to create a learning community for students.

- Be visible. Keep up appearances. Maintain professionalism and keep the "main thing the main thing," as Stephen Covey says in *First Things First* (1994). Concentrate on student learning.

- Remember this is a process. It will be resolved one way or the other. But remember that people in schools have long memories. Whatever happens during this time will be remembered until all the players have retired. Stories get repeated as part of the culture so concentrate on doing your job but remain neutral. Stay focused on students.

Summary

"Don't think that happiness will be possible only when conditions around you become perfect. Happiness lies in your own heart" (Hanh, 1998, p. 250).

Dealing with staff is an intricate ballet of support and conflict. It is important to have management skills in both. Develop some skills in listening and in conflict mediation. Develop questioning skills that help adults discover their own gifts. Effective leadership and management in dealing with staff "lie in your own heart."

Personal Journal

1. What are some of my strengths in showing support for my staff?

2. What are some process skills I need to learn in dealing with conflict?

3. What gift did I receive in dealing with a recent issue of conflict? What gift did I receive in dealing with a recent instance of support?

Group Discussion

1. How do the traits of a leader, such as Culture Builder and Character Builder from McEwan, interact with the need for management strategies?

2. McEwan describes an instructional leader as an Educator. Discuss how that role interacts with the above strategies on dealing with staff.

4

Discipline as a Leadership Tool

Parker J. Palmer opened his book *The Courage to Teach* (1998) with the powerful statement: "I am a teacher at heart, and there are moments in the classroom when I can hardly hold the joy." Do you remember that incredible feeling of having students "get it"?

One of the joys for me as a high school administrator was that as certain students would walk across the stage at graduation, shake hands, and receive their diploma, I knew that it would not have happened without my support or intervention. Knowing that I made a difference in the lives of students still sustains me when times are difficult. Those are the moments that give such joy that I can hardly explain the feeling.

It is important to remember that one of the reasons we chose education as a career was because we wanted to make a difference in the lives of young people. As an administrator and leader, that is still the vision—what we do changes the world, one child at a time, which is why it is important to look at guidelines and interactions with our students. As a school leader, some of those opportunities to interact with students revolve around discipline.

Discipline as a Leadership Opportunity

Discipline is not merely management; it is a leadership tool as well. Looking at discipline as leadership means looking at how the shaping of behavior is as educational as learning the three R's. It is our task as adults and educators to help students understand why they act as they do and to help them make wiser choices to shape future actions.

We too often equate discipline with punishment. Punishment, however, relates to power and force. In his book *Teacher Effectiveness Training* (2003), Dr. Thomas Gordon said, "power [is] disguised as 'authority,' and power is terribly destructive in human relationships" (pp. 200–201). Punishment works as long as the punisher is perceived as being bigger or stronger. Plus, the efficacy of punishment as an external force decreases as students get older. For example, a three-year-old may need to be concerned about mom or dad's reaction if the child ventures out of the yard. The child needs to realize that a time-out is a possible outcome. The isolation of a time-out is a punishment that works. However, time-outs seldom work as punishment for teenagers. Time-outs may be helpful if a situation has to be calmed down and some time is needed. What works more with teenagers is to be able to talk out why the behavior is inappropriate and what can happen better next time. Fear of a parent is not as productive in shaping behavior at this age, as is respect, or the loss of it, if a teenager breaks the rules.

Robert Marzano wrote a book entitled *Classroom Management That Works* (2003). In Marzano's meta-analysis of management strategies, he learned that "Clearly, the research supports the notion that designing and implementing rules and procedures in class and even at home has a profound impact on student behavior and on student learning. However, research also indicates that rules and procedures should not simply be imposed on students. Rather, the proper design of rules and procedures involves explanation and group input" (p. 16).

At the administrative level that means "a well-managed school is so important to the achievement of students that it has been identified as a national goal" (p. 104). An effective school leader facilitates the clear expectations at the school level, which are translated into the clear expectations and management at the classroom level. Again, Marzano (2003), "in short, an emphasis on the effective management of the school in general is as important as individual classroom management and may even be a bigger determinant of the climate of the school than the aggregate impact of the management in individual classrooms" (p. 106). Leadership in the area of behavioral expectations is a key force in effective management of a safe school.

Marzano described action steps for leaders at the school level. One, establish rules and procedures for behavioral problems that might be caused by the school's physical characteristics or the school's routines. Take care of scheduling if it creates problems. Have classes released at different times so that crowded hallways do not precipitate opportunities for bad behavior. Decrease travel time. Have shorter passing times so students do not get in trouble. Have more supervision in congested hallways.

Two, establish clear schoolwide rules and procedures regarding specific types of misbehavior. It is important that students understand the expectations and the consequences of behavior. It is particularly helpful to have student groups be part of the discussions so that they have ownership of the rules. If there is an issue, it is particularly helpful to get student input. For example, guests from other schools at school dances have caused some problems. What would be the best way to deal with this? The first reaction is to stop all guests, but that harms those who did the right thing. Instead, bring in some student leaders and maybe even a person who brought a guest that caused difficulty and generate possible solutions. There are such things as guest registrations, carrying Ids, or limiting guests to certain dances such as Homecoming and the Prom.

Three, establish and enforce appropriate consequences for specific types of misbehavior. It is important that consequences are tied to the offense and are seen as meaningful. For example, in the research, Saturday School was found to be an effective deterrent, if used as a time for restitution and learning new behavior. The efficacy of suspensions is questionable. What suspensions do is allow for cooling off and the ability to restore calm in a school. The verdict is out as to whether suspension changes bad behavior, unless there is an educational component with the student upon return.

Again use student discussion groups to talk about some possibilities. Opening a dialogue between students, parents, and staff about some of the issues helps get differing viewpoints on the table.

Four, establish a system that allows for the early detection of students who have high potential for violence and extreme behaviors. It is important that an administrator stay current on studies about warning signs for future extreme behavior. For example, any "form of violent fighting appears to be a strong indicator that future problems might appear. Additionally, harassment and nonviolent misbehavior might indicate future problems" (Marzano, 2003, p. 113). It is important not to be fatalistic and deterministic, but it is important to use relationships with staff, students, and parents to be honest and to not try to soft pedal some behaviors that are known to be precursors to more serious events.

It is important to offer services, suggest other resources, and hold students accountable for their behavior. If the behavior is minimized because consequences are also minimized, the behavior will not be taken seriously. We do students and families a disservice when that happens.

We know that bullying and harassment, for example, must be taken seriously. We know that students who have been victimized have a tendency to victimize others and themselves. They are more likely to become bullies and to experience depression. We know from the research on school shootings that those who resort to violence in this extreme were also victims of violence during their short lives.

Therefore, an effective leader establishes clear expectations and guidelines that shape the behavioral climate of a school. Such expectations are then carried out at the classroom level, which helps create a system where everyone knows the boundaries and the consequences for stepping over those boundaries.

Process for Discipline

Gordon (2003) described the necessary process of discipline in terms of classroom behavior with teachers and students, but the same method works for building level interactions between administrators and students, as well.

The following process is what he called a Method III, which is based on a flow of respect between student and adult, using two-way communication, and deriving a solution that is acceptable to both. It is very similar to the process used by Fisher et al. (1991) and the one described by Sigford in *Who Said School Administration Would Be Fun* (2005).

The process is:

- Define the problem. Use active listening and "I" messages to get to the real problem.
- Generate possible solutions. List possible solutions without putting an evaluative overlay on them. Do not require students to justify their ideas—this is a brainstorming session.
- Evaluate the solutions. Explore the consequences for each of the solutions. Use open-ended questions to get the student to come to an understanding about the benefits or consequences of the solutions.
- Make the decision. Seek input from the student(s) about the best decision. Work toward agreement that this is truly the best decision.

Caveat: Consensus does not always work. In a majority vote or consensus, someone is giving in to what Simon in Larry Cuban (2001) calls "satisficing" (p. 12). In order to "satisfy" someone, another must "sacrifice" his or her opinion.

- Work toward agreement.
- Determine how to implement the decision. Ask each party what they are willing to do to make the decision work. Write down what each person agrees to do and have each party sign it. Committing in writing is more potent than a verbal agreement; the resolution is more likely to "stick."
- Assess the success of the solution. Make an appointment with the student(s) in a week to meet to see how it's going (Gordon, 2003, pp. 228–236). By committing to a follow-up, the student understands that you, too, are committed to resolution. You are committed to changing behavior.

Be sure to keep that appointment and ask the student(s) how it's going. If going well, remind the students of the process and what was learned so they can use the tools again. That is discipline because it is teaching. If the solution is not working, generate other possible ideas that may be more workable. Either way, the student learns that discipline is a process and it is about changing behavior, not about who is older, stronger, or louder.

Other Important Guidelines That Help Establish Discipline as Leadership

- **Be fair.** When working with students, it is important to use discipline codes as *guidelines*. Equity and fairness do not mean equal. Every child who throws paper in a classroom does not get the same consequence because situations are different. Every child who runs in the hall is not suspended.

An administrator must use sound judgment in making decisions about discipline. If discipline codes were to be enforced without thought, then a clerk or robot could look at the discipline codes and administer the consequence. However, the administrator must look at the situation and the student to make the decision that helps shape behavior. Discipline is meant to be a process, not an end.

It is true that administering discipline as education takes more time than merely handing out consequences. However, it is timesaving in the long run because, when students learn strategies to control behavior, recidivism will decrease.

Teachers must also understand that when a student is sent to the office out of the class, the teacher abdicates the right to determine the consequence. It is then up to the administrator to make the best decision for the student. **About 90% of the discipline referrals come from 10% of teachers** (Whitaker, 1999). Whitaker continues, "many times, the building leader spends a disproportionate amount of time reacting to problems sent by difficult teachers. . . . Stopping this long line of office referrals from just a few staff members without being viewed as unsupportive of teachers is essential for effective instructional leadership" (p. 9).

The other 90% of teachers deal with their own discipline issues because they, too, understand that discipline is a process and is best handled as a function of a relationship, and that the best way for a student to learn about behavior is in the context of where the behavior occurred. Sending a student to the office is reminiscent of the old means of discipline—"Just wait until your father gets home." Comments such as those are based on the punishment model. By the number of persons in our prisons, we refuse to learn that punishment does not work.

- **Effective discipline is based on relationships.** Punishment is about meting out consequences, which can be done outside the context of relationships. Judges can sentence criminals without ever knowing them. Then it feels like punishment is done TO them.

However, effective discipline is done WITH someone. It is done in the context of relationships, how the behavior affected the greater good of the classroom, school, or individual. It is done in how a behavior hurt a relationship. True discipline gives the person an opportunity to repair that important relationship. An important question to the offender is to say, "What can you do to fix the relationship? How can you restore the trust?"

Not only is effective discipline based on relationships, but relationships also are "important because students are more likely to make a personal commitment to engage in rigorous learning when they know that teachers, parents, and other students actually care how well they do (Successful Practices Network). High schools that go from being good schools to being great understand that "the key was that their work in relationship-building seemed to be driven by guiding principals, such as respect, responsibility, honesty, trustworthiness, compassion, loyalty, optimism, adaptability, courage, contemplation, initiative, and perseverance" (p. 28). Relationships matter in conducting discipline, in establishing rigor, and establishing a learning community.

• **There is no such thing as a perfect discipline policy.** Because true discipline is based on relationship and process, there is no way that a document or list of rules can describe all the issues. Discipline policies are fear- and power-based, and external, as opposed to being educational. Discipline policies talk about penalties and consequences imposed upon the individual. People believe discipline policies are a solution to a problem, when in fact they are guidelines in dealing with a dilemma.

A discipline policy should be used as a guideline, not as a line in the sand. Use the policy to talk about the severity of the behavior, but do not use it to create a power struggle. The only way to win a power struggle is to stay out of one. Because students are experts in enticing adults into power struggles, adults need to be smart enough to stay out of them.

When working with older students, teach them how to stay out of power struggles. A physical illustration to students of what happens in a power struggle is to have a student stand, facing the administrator. Ask the student to use one hand to push on the administrator's shoulder. (Usually, they are hesitant to do this and will only touch gently.) Ask them to do it again and push harder.

Then ask, "What happened when you pushed on me?" It is obvious that the administrator braced and physically pushed back.

Now ask the student to do it again. Before he is able to push, sidestep so that he is literally pushing on air. Then ask, "What happened?" Obviously, when there was nothing to push against, the student loses balance. When someone sidesteps a power struggle, the other person loses. Power struggles set up occasions where one person pushes and another pushes back. The force increases each time a person pushes.

However, the moral of the physical example is to show students the effects of a power struggle. Then, work with the students to help them see how they created a verbal push and how the other person pushed back (hopefully verbally). Help them understand how they could have "sidestepped" so that the power struggle did not occur.

This is a valuable lesson to give adults as well. Sometimes adults put themselves in a corner, and they do not know how to get out without "losing face." Too often adults are afraid to back down because they fear that will make them look weak. The opposite is often true. If an adult processes what is happening, relates from the heart, and describes what is happening, there is no need for one-upmanship. No need to fall flat on one's face!

- **Safety Issues.** When safety is at stake, either personal or building, the administrator has no option but to apply the appropriate consequences, which may involve applying punishment. Students involved in fights are suspended. Students who bring weapons to school are expelled. Students who set fires are suspended, possibly referred for testing in special education, or possibly moved to more restricted settings.

There is no option when it comes to safety, although there are still opportunities for education to shape behavior.

- **Know your state laws, including special education rules and laws.** It is important to be conversant with state laws, Web sites, rules for special education, truancy laws and programs, etc. when it comes to discipline.

Sadly, there will be times when building relationships or using discipline as a learning tool will not work. The student may be mentally ill or the behavior may be so ingrained that it cannot change. The administrator must then know what steps to take next. Use outside resources to help. Special education directors, social workers, police liaisons, counselors, and the courts are all tools that we have to use at some time or another.

Another resource is a book by Louis Rosen, *School Discipline: Best Practice for Administrators* (2005). The book describes how to establish a discipline code, how to help teachers conduct their own discipline, and how to understand laws.

Harassment and Bullying

Harassment and bullying are important, separate discipline issues that must be taken very seriously. We know that students who are victims of harassment are more likely to commit suicide or suffer depression.

There is a book, *Our Guys* (1997) by Bernard Lefkowitz, which was used as source material for an episode of the television program *Law and Order* and as the plot for a made-for-television movie. Young men, who happened to be athletes, brutally victimized a mentally handicapped young woman. The behavior was excused by the town. The boys had committed prior acts of harassment and bullying, but no one had intervened. In fact, their behavior had been excused by the theory that "boys will be boys." Plus, they were athletes and were not held to the same standards as other students. The boys did not feel that there would be consequences for their behavior and they assaulted and raped a young, mentally diminished girl who wanted their approval, attention, and regard.

The book was a real-life poignant example of what happened when bullying and harassment were not treated as serious. We cannot avoid, ignore, or disregard harassment or bullying. We must intervene at early instances so that the behavior does not escalate to the point that people are hurt even more severely.

We know that the statistics about the numbers of students who are harassed in schools are astonishing. We have learned that demeaning comments, undue teasing, or other bullying behavior are predictors of later more serious behaviors, unless there is intervention and education. Harassment and bullying behaviors contribute to racism, to harassment of students with disabilities, to harassment of students with sexual orientation other than heterosexual, and to a climate in a building that is other than safe, welcoming, and supportive.

We also know that most victims of harassment and bullying will say that too often adults watch and do not intervene. We, as adults, MUST intervene. As administrators, we must create an atmosphere that does what Marzano (2003) describes as "establish[ing] a system that allows for the early detection of students who have high potentials for violence and extreme behaviors" (p. 113). Bullying and harassment are behaviors that have that potential.

This is particularly important in dealing with our boys. The literature has begun talking about how boys are left behind in schools. Paul D. Slocumb, Ed.D, in his book *Hear Our Cry: Boys in Crisis* (2004), stated, "females now outnumber males in the acquisition of a college degree" (p. 6). However, boys commit 95% of the juvenile homicides. They are the perpetrators in four out of five crimes that end up in juvenile court. Boys are more likely to be referred to the office for discipline as they lag behind in reading and writing. They are more likely to be suspended from school and are more often qualified for special education services. They are bullied, and they bully in return (p. 6). It is important to pay attention as an educational leader to the establishment of fair discipline practices and to use every opportunity to educate and shape behavior.

With most discipline issues, students start the school year with a relatively clean slate. However, in some states the harassment violations are cumulative. Schools must increase the consequences with repeated offenses because this behavior must be taken seriously.

When students who have been victimizing other students are sent to the office, it is important to have them describe at an age appropriate level what happened, help them understand the consequences of their behavior, how it hurt them and others, and then help them understand the consequences. It is also important that they understand there are legal ramifications, and these ramifications become more severe if the behavior happens again. But what is most important in order to help them is for them to learn other tools to deal with situations that are frustrating.

Throughout this process, especially for our boys, it is important for them to understand and verbalize how harassment and bullying FEEL. Slocumb (2004) discussed how the language skills of females mature more quickly than for males. Consequently, males do not have the word tools to describe their feelings; instead, they act them out. "This lack of language sets up most males to be largely disconnected emotionally" (Slocumb, p. 17). "Without an emotional language, empathy does not exist. Without empathy, conscience can't develop. Without a conscience, there is little sense of right and wrong. Without a sense of right and wrong, boundaries don't exist. Without boundaries, it's very difficult to articulate a personal code of ethics or have a sense of integrity. Without ethics and integrity, words are limited. Frustration turns to anger, and anger turns to rage. The result is raw, misdirected energy with few words" (Slocumb, p. 23). It is what Slocumb called "an emotional abyss" (p. 23).

It is very important to work with parents and students to help correct all inappropriate behavior, particularly with harassment and bullying. It is equally important that parents understand what happened, why it is wrong, and what will happen clearly if the behavior repeats. It is important to help the parents discover other tools for children to learn.

One possible educational tool for administrators is to prepare some educational materials to be used with students at an age-appropriate level. For all students, it is important to discuss these issues with parents face-to-face. In addition, one can prepare a question-and-answer sheet about simple facts of harassment. Older students can take information home and discuss the facts with their parents. Require that the student return to the office the next day with the question-and-answer sheet signed by the parent to show that the student had to spend time discussing this with the parent.

If appropriate, the educational leader can develop a contract that the student has to sign which states that "I, ——————, understand that my behavior was inappropriate. If it happens again, _____ [describe the specific consequences here]." Have the student sign it, date it. Make a copy for the student, for the parent, and for your files. Then, mail the copy home to the parent so that everyone is very clear about the consequences.

It is equally important to work with students to help them describe how behavior and actions make them FEEL. Help them figure out ways to describe the feelings so that the feelings can be dealt with, not acted out.

Ways to Prevent the Need for Discipline or Punishment

It is simplistic, but true, that the development of relationships decreases bad behavior. Students and teachers truly want to do the right thing. They are motivated by positive interactions and positive esteem from others. I do not know where this came from, but was once told that all it takes for a student to be engaged in school is to know that ONE adult cares. The corollary is that students who do not graduate from high school or who are disconnected believe that there has never been any ONE person who believed in them, mentored them, or supported them in the school environment. It only takes ONE.

Some strategies that are helpful in creating a culture that promotes healthy relationships and healthy choices are as follows:

- **Think of each student as though he or she were your own child.** When an administrator thinks of a child as though that person was a relative, it changes the interaction. If students are friends or loved ones, it is more likely that they will be treated with respect and according to the Golden Rule. It is also helpful to remember that every child is the beloved son or daughter of some parent who truly wants the best.

- **Remember the purpose of education.** As decisions are made by staff, and even in discipline, remember what is in the best interests of the student. It is not about what is easiest or most convenient for the teacher.

If a teacher becomes engaged in a power struggle with a student because the student did not stay after school and the teacher only stays after school on Thursday, then school is about what is best for the adult, not the learning of the student. It is important to work with both teacher and student to come to a decision that facilitates the learning for the child.

If a child acts up in a teacher's class and the teacher wants the child removed, it is important to help the student understand the behavior and its consequences. It is also important to work with the teacher to give them alternative strategies in dealing with behavior. The first important tool is to help the teacher relate to the student as a human being.

- **Greet students in the morning.** Be outside when the buses come or be in the lobby. Be in the halls. Be visible to them and greet students. Get to know kids by name and use the names. Notice when students have a haircut, a new shirt, or if they look particularly nice.

Create an atmosphere where the teachers will do the same. The more students interact positively with adults, the more they can learn appropriate self-regulatory behaviors.

- **Be visible with students.** Be in the lunchroom, hallways, at activities. By being there, students will know you care. Have students involved on action committees in the school. Students should be on advisory committees, curriculum committees, and district goal committees.

- **Create opportunities to interact in a positive manner.** Some administrators create student advisory committees or they chair student council so that students have an opportunity to have a voice in the school. Student councils work at every grade level, from elementary to secondary. Listen to student concerns and use their expertise to help solve issues. For example, if students are making a mess in the bathroom, go to the committee and ask for ways to address the issue. Not only will they generate possible ideas, but it will also create the knowledge that they will share with other students that they need to be neater in the bathrooms. Peer pressure is important. It is important to give credibility and power to student leaders so they can create ownership in their school.

- **Know what is going on in the classrooms.** Know what students are learning. It is an opportunity to ask students if they got their art project done or if they finished reading a certain book. If you, as administrator, can use that to talk to students, you are opening up the opportunity for a relationship and, importantly, you are demonstrating the importance of learning. You are involved as an instructional leader.

- **Establish relationships with the community and students.** In its annual survey about public opinion concerning schools, Phi Delta Kappa asks parents about their perceptions of their school and schools across the nation. Repeatedly, parents rate their school highly and other schools lower. Schools are often the heart of a community, particularly in smaller communities. It is the place where the community comes to hear concerts, watch athletic activities, or take community education classes.

One school in rural northern Minnesota opens its building seven days a week so people can use the computer labs and access the Internet. Many small communities use their libraries to access the Internet, but in this case their public library was a traveling bookmobile. The economy is depressed and the Internet access provided some adults the opportunity to take online classes to improve their skills and look for other jobs. The school truly became the focal point of the community.

Use students to enhance this connection. Have students sit on advisory committees so they provide fresh insight and build liaisons. Sometimes there is a permanent high school student member to the Board of Education. Plus, the student body is then seen as a true team player because they are represented and more connected to the workings of the district as well as to the high school.

Older students make good mentors for younger students. Work across levels so that high school students can tutor younger ones. It truly takes a village to raise a child and if all children are well educated, the village is a better place to live.

Successful relationships with students are key to a principal's successful relationship with the community, and therefore, fundamental to a principal's perceived effectiveness. Students go home and talk to their parents—hopefully. The relationship an administrator has with students is directly related to the perceived effectiveness of the administrator by the community. If a principal is seen as fair and caring, community members will act that way too. If a principal uses opportunities to get students involved with the community, the community respects the principal's desires for connectedness.

Summary

In real estate, the key to a prime property is location, location, location. In education, the key to an effective school leader is student, student, student. It is about educating our students as a prime commodity, as key to our cumulative future. It is about using discipline as a leadership strategy to educate and shape behaviors in a school and in the greater community. It is about teaching students and adults how some choices destroy relationships, and how those choices destroy the spider web of human connections. When that happens, we are all diminished. When we deepen human connections, we are all strengthened.

Such relationships were like those described about the Ya-Yas in Rebecca Wells' books about true friends. In her most recent book *Ya-Yas in Bloom* (2005), Wells said it well:

"Nothing mattered except that they had found one another. In the whole wide world, they had found true sister-friends" (p. 34).

Personal Journal

1. What is different in thinking about discipline as leadership, as opposed to thinking of it as punishment?

2. Am I less likely to be patient and understanding when I am pressured for time or tired or stressed? What are some strategies I can use to counteract that?

3. What are my strengths in dealing with discipline issues? What are my hot buttons? How can I work around those?

Group Discussion

1. How can an educational leader work with staff to understand that there is no such thing as a perfect discipline policy? That discipline is a dilemma, not a problem?

2. Identify the people on the staff that are the most effective in dealing with student issues. Is there a way to utilize their expertise to provide some professional development for the staff? Are there global strategies that can be used for training on a professional development day or as part of a staff meeting?

3. Is there a way to use the analysis of data, the numbers of students sent to the office and for what offenses, to get the staff involved in looking at discipline as education?

5

School as Heart and Soul of a Community

Leaders recognize that a meaningful relationship with the greater community is as important as the relationships within a building. Parents entrust their children—their dearest commodity—to the care of teachers and schools. Consequently, it is important to recognize that parents can be our greatest allies. Just about every administrator knows this but also recognizes that it is difficult to accomplish this goal for several reasons. One, new parents are constantly coming to school so one must be aware of bringing new parents up to speed. An administrator has to repeat items every year for the new parents and yet move the experienced parents along. This can be a source of burnout for some administrators because it is difficult to stay fresh in repeating the same information year after year.

Two, we all recognize that no one will ever say there was TOO MUCH communication. No matter how many newsletters, emails, telephone calls, hand-outs, faxes, or voice mails are delivered, there will always be someone who said, "I did not see/hear/read it. How was I to know this?" Besides, as parents are inundated with more and more information, they, like us, learn to skim for information and sometimes forget that they read, saw, or heard about an item unless they wrote it down on the calendar immediately.

Three, communication with stakeholders is a different type of skill than communication within a building. Administrators need different strategies in order to accomplish that goal.

Relationships with the community, in the current climate of school choice with vouchers, charter schools, and home schools, become even more crucial because parents have many options. Plus, in our climate of choice, more and more parents are acting as though schools are Old Country Buffet, a restaurant that offers many choices from which the diner can pick and choose. We have parents who want to have their child come to school for electives but go to another school for required courses. Therefore, the relationship with parents and community is vital because we want parents to choose us.

Relationships With Parents

1. It is the responsibility of us all. It is important that all members of the organization realize that it is important to develop healthy relationships with parents. Teachers and administrators share the responsibility of establishing and maintaining open and frequent communications with parents. Communication is more than just parent conferences and curriculum nights; it is the attitude that parents and school people are partners. The effective school leader both models that behavior and helps the staff understand that as well.

Our community members talk at soccer games or church events about what happens in schools. It is important that that talk is positive.

2. Use technology to maintain a dialogue and to share information. Many schools use Web sites to post school newsletters and other information that all parents need to know. Some schools use blanket emails for subscribers to send home alerts, such as for announcements, conference times, and school closings due to weather.

Individual teachers may use a password-protected system so parents may access a child's attendance, grades, and even what a child has chosen for lunch. Individual teachers have Web sites where they post weekly assignments and tasks.

At first, teachers were fearful that having all that information available would increase parental intrusion into what is happening in the classroom. What has happened in some schools is just the opposite. One teacher said that because parents were so informed, she had the best conferences she had ever had because they could talk about real issues.

Sometimes administrators will have to make certain that the use of technology is not prejudicial to those who cannot afford it. It is unwise to assume that its use is available to all parents; if someone does not have access, other methods of information-sharing should be used in a manner that is respectful and not judgmental.

Some parents will use the public library for Internet access. Other parents will need to have hard copies mailed to their homes. Some will need notification the "old-fashioned way"—by telephone. It is important to have a variety of approaches and to do so in a way that is not condescending or demeaning to parents who may not have Internet access.

3. Open houses, parent conferences, curriculum nights, concerts, plays. Open houses, parent conferences and curriculum nights are opportunities for teachers and staff to shine. Teachers are able to demonstrate their knowledge of content and students. It is even the opportunity for the custodian to be proud of a sparklingly clean building.

Parents use the time with administrators to discuss concerns that are not as easily discussed on the telephone. For example, a parent asked to visit with the administrator because of some concerns regarding bullying behavior directed toward their adopted, Asian child. The administrator knew nothing about this behavior because the child was afraid to complain, and culturally, that was not familiar behavior. The administrator listened and then spent the next two days dealing with the behavior and found, indeed, that some bad behavior had been occurring. The behavior was dealt with, and consequences were applied to the bad actors.

Administrators need to help teachers develop effective parent conferencing strategies. Teachers, particularly new teachers, are fearful of parent conferences because they fear being criticized. Training programs rarely provide training in conducting successful conferences. As a leader, one important management strategy in working with new staff is to provide training prior to parent conferences.

Following are a few suggestions for effective parent conferences:

- **Nonstudent related issues.** Sometimes a parent will bring up issues that are personal and not related to the child. A bitter divorce. Complaints about another teacher. Complaining about the district, for example. If the teacher has time, be a polite listener. It is important to use empathic, active listening but understand that sometimes a person just needs to vent. If the teacher knows of resources, one could suggest them. Try to tie the stories back to the issue of the student's progress. If there is no time, this is a time to suggest other resources.

- **Be sure to know the students.** It is terribly embarrassing, and has happened too often, that a teacher has told a parent, "I really do not know your child that well, but his or her grades are . . ." Such a comment is absolutely inexcusable.
- **Begin the conference with some personal attribute about the student.** "Xiong is a focused student. Jose is always prepared." Then give other information.
- **Do not just repeat the report card.** Parents want to know how their child is DOING. Talk about the strengths of the child as well as what the student needs to work on.
- **Ask the parents if they have any concerns.** By soliciting information from the parents, the teacher will learn a different side of the child and will be able to develop a deeper understanding and a sharper relationship with that student.
- **Be honest, but not critical, about student progress.** "Dimitri seems to answer only the first part of a question. He would get better grades if he would expand his ideas. What has worked with you at home to get him to do that?"
- **Parent conferences are often too short, particularly at the secondary level.** However, waiting parents get upset if their time is minimized because someone else took too long.
- **Some teachers have tried purchasing unobtrusive timers to keep things moving.** "I understand that we could talk a lot more. But in order to be respectful of all parents, we need to wrap up our meeting here tonight. Just as you had to wait, there are others waiting too. If you have further concerns, email me or telephone me so we can discuss them in depth. Here is my email and telephone . . ." Give parents an opportunity to continue the dialogue if necessary yet be respectful of others who may be waiting.

Any opportunity to be visible and in dialogue with parents strengthens the home/school partnership.

4. Volunteers. Parent volunteers are a rich resource for any building leader. The more that parents are involved in their child's education, the more successful we will all be. Volunteers can be used in many areas. They can be used on playgrounds, in the media center, for registration, for tutoring, as chaperones, or in many other capacities.

It is important for the leader to put adults into positions where they can be successful. Provide training if necessary. For example, if a group of volunteers are helping the English Language Learners (ELL) students, the leader should provide some training for them on effective literacy strategies. This way they will feel like they have the tools to make a difference and that what they are doing is important.

It will also be important to provide some training for the teachers in how to use a volunteer effectively. A volunteer needs to feel like a part of the team so the teacher needs to give the volunteer an assigned, important task to complete. It cannot be "busy work" just to keep a disruptive student occupied. Some teachers develop folders that are kept in a certain place with set tasks with a student's name on them that a volunteer can pick up without disrupting a class. It is important, however, for the teacher to establish a relationship with the volunteer. Volunteers want to know that what they are doing matters. (It's about relationships.) So the teacher may need to take a few minutes during a transition to hear from the volunteer about the progress. Or the teacher and volunteer may develop a written feedback system and plan to meet on a biweekly basis so there is some face-to-face interaction that will keep the volunteer coming back.

It is important to keep volunteers in areas where data privacy is not breached. For example, volunteers should not be filing into cummulative folders. Also, be careful of volunteers in the main office because they may hear things or see things that are covered by the Data Practices Act.

5. Develop a repertoire of parent-involvement activities. In his book *You Have to Go to School—You're the Principal! 101 Tips to Make It Better for Your Students, Your Staff, and Yourself* (2004), Paul Young suggests developing a repertoire of parent-involvement activities. The suggestions range from "donuts for dads, muffins for moms" days, to grandparent, grandfriend days, to videos and recordings of curriculum nights for parents to check out (p. 112). The types of activities are not necessarily important. What is important is that there is frequency and variety so that all parents can be included over time.

6. Relationships with parents who do not come to school. For a variety of reasons some parents do not come to school. We too often interpret that as someone who does not care about the child's progress. Erase this thought. We have to assume that all parents care about a child's progress but that there are other issues in place that prevent them from coming to the school.

It is important to find out why the parents do not want to come to school. Have they had bad experiences previously with school? Do they feel unwelcome? Do they lack transportation? Are they working two jobs and cannot take time off? Do they see it as unimportant?

There are many reasons why parents do not come to school. Parents, first of all, need to feel that the school is indeed a community school and that they are welcome to come. They need to feel a connection with someone in the building, that the teacher is happy to see them, that the principal knows who they are, and that other parents are friendly and welcoming.

Some parents do not understand how to "do" school. Their childhood experiences may not have been positive so it will be important for the school leader to invite them personally, go to their house/apartment, or any other idea for a direct contact.

Parents of students who are not always successful in school sometimes stop coming because they are tired of being judged as being lousy parents. They are tired of hearing bad news. They have probably tried to do everything they know how to do and have run out of strategies. Some of these parents are missing some tools in their toolkit of effective parenting. They avoid having their failures pointed out again and again.

One strategy to reengage them is to find something positive about the child and call the parents prior to conferences with the good news. While on the telephone, invite the parents to come to conferences but make certain they are not "sandbagged" with bad news once they arrive.

With older students whose parents have stopped coming, it may be necessary to work with the student personally. As an administrator, one can work with the student to talk about progress, wishes, and how to make those dreams come true. Help the student become a self-advocate. Hook him up with resources such as the school counselor to develop some plans for postsecondary.

Some students do not have parents available. The days of Ozzie and Harriet are over—if they ever occurred. Children live in a wide variety of family configurations. Some have both parents; some have one. Some have extended families; some are living on their own. Some live with two moms or dads; some have none.

If a student does not have an adult to come to conferences, no matter how old the child is, we can begin to give them skills that lead to resilience. We, as educators, can begin to help the child assess personal strengths, establish goals, and then build connections to make those goals happen. Students do not need two biological parents in order to be successful. It's nice, but it is not reality for many of our students. If students have ONE adult who cares about them, whether that adult is related or not, then students can be successful as long as there are relationships to build from. Help establish those connections.

7. Relationships with parents who are of a different culture. For some of our newer immigrant families, language and cultural barriers prevent them from coming to school because they are embarrassed, fearful, nervous, or a combination of all of the above. Here are some strategies to use in working with immigrant families.

A. Some of our immigrant families have never had to have parent conferences, so they do not know what is expected. As a leader, go to them early on to develop relationships, begin to tell them about conferences, and give them a personal invitation.

   Go to them. If there is a church, or community room in an apartment building, or central gathering place, the administrator can go to them at the beginning of the school year to start developing relationships.

B. Provide day care. Many families have other children at home and may not know someone who can provide child care. Invite the parents to bring their other children. Work with the high school and the National Honor Society for students to provide in-house child care. The hours can also be used for the Honor Society students for their community service hours.

C. Provide meals. Some families are working two jobs, both at meager wages. They are putting in long hours. Work with PTA to provide dinner for the families so they can come on a break from work or between jobs.

D. Provide transportation. Some churches are willing to help by providing vans for transportation. Or write for grants with local foundations to provide transportation.

E. Provide interpreters. It is usually not a good idea to use a child as an interpreter. Children often pick up English faster than the parents. But in many cultures, using the child as "expert" inverts the normal order where parents are to be respected for their knowledge. Instead, use local interpreter agencies to hire someone. When using an interpreter, be sure to train the teachers to speak to the parent, not the interpreter.

When communicating with parents of different cultures, there are some strategies that are important to remember.

- Speak slowly. Do not talk as though someone is deaf, but slow down the pace so that a person would be able to translate as they go. Anyone who has learned a second, or third, language understands that it takes time to think about the word in the new language to connect it with a word in the old language. As a person becomes more skilled in the language, it is not always necessary to translate every word because the person learns the meaning of the word on its own.

- Keep sentences short. It is difficult to make meaning from long sentences when one is learning a language. Simple sentences are best.

Write things down. Many families have someone who can read for them whether in the church or apartment complex. Even if someone cannot read English, or cannot read it well, they often have a resource that can help. It is less embarrassing for them to ask a friend, neighbor, or sponsor to translate, than it is to ask the principal or teacher. Plus, the written note provides a record, a reference point, in case they forget the exact information (Pipher, 2002, pp. 353–354).

8. Negative Parents. Not all parent interactions are positive. In fact, administrators will say that the increasing demands by, and negativity of, parents is increasing overall. They will say that that is one of the key factors in deciding to leave administration for retirement or for other positions where they do not have to deal with such constant pressures. We know that the statistics about the numbers of students who are harassed in schools are astonishing.

An excellent resource for administrators is Elaine K. McEwan's book, *How to Deal With Parents Who Are Angry, Troubled, Afraid, or Just Plain Crazy* that was published in 1998. She described a sample of parents of today as:

- Less respectful of authority
- More educated about schools and view schools as another "consumable"
- Cynical and distrustful

McEwan (1998) has some strategies to cope with these increasingly splintered demands:

- Be trustworthy. Be a person of values and explain them. Do the right thing for the right reason. Parents may not agree with you, but over time they will know that you are dealing with a bigger issue.

- Have integrity. An administrator makes decisions based on values and a concern for all.
- Welcome parents to your office. McEwan advises shaking hands but that is not always appropriate for certain cultures, depending on male/female interactions. But one can create a welcoming atmosphere without physical contact.
- Sit eye-to-eye and knee-to-knee—Again these ideas are not necessarily appropriate for non-Western, mixed-gender settings. However, a person can sit so that there is a connection. Do not sit behind the desk because that makes an automatic barrier. Sit so that people are comfortable and can have a meaningful conversation.
- Listen. This strategy is one that can be used across cultures and across genders. It may take some ability to listen with the heart, to ask questions of interpreters, and to be willing to be patient.
- Open your mind. It is important to listen to the parent as though you were the person speaking. It is important to see the issue from their perspective and to demonstrate that you, as an administrator, truly hear their viewpoint. You may disagree with it, or have more information to add from a different perspective, but it is important to be responsive to the presentation of the issues.
- Keep calm; be confident.
- Establish time limits.
- Apologize, if appropriate. Sometimes people do things out of ignorance or lack of knowledge about another culture. It is okay to admit the error.
- Get to the point.
- Empathize.
- Ask questionsSpeak gently.
- Redirect.
- Lower the boom lightly.
- Welcome constructive criticism.
- Don't react.
- Take your time.
- Don't tell—show.
- Give options.
- Focus on the issue, not on personalities. (pp. 25–37)

Relationships With the Greater Community

A successful relationship with the community can make or break an administrator. The first place to start building that relationship is in developing a strong, visible, positive relationship with students, as described in Chapter 4.

Apart from student relationships, some principals belong to community organizations such as the Rotary Club or Chamber of Commerce to build community relationships. It is more common for high school principals and superintendents to do this than it is for elementary and even middle-level principals. Community organizations offer a valuable way to educate the community, particularly the business community, about finance issues, bond issues, legislative concerns, and so on.

It is also a way to build connections that lead to possible volunteers for the schools. Corporations sometimes want to volunteer as part of their mission. It is much easier to call someone that is familiar than it is to make cold calls. Those connections prove to be invaluable in ways no one ever imagines.

For example, several organizations, churches, and a major company involved in the food industry, have as part of their mission to be involved in the community and to give to those less fortunate. They wanted to volunteer in the schools, particularly with the immigrant community. However, many felt inadequate, untrained, and surprised about the skills necessary in dealing with the many cultures found in school.

We developed a partnership with a local university who had a teacher training certification on learning about diverse perspectives. We created a module to train the trainers for key volunteers in several organizations to learn about diverse learners and learning strategies. The trainers would then be responsible to train volunteers each year so that the program can continue in a manner that benefits us all. It was truly exciting to watch.

We then trained the volunteers in literacy strategies so they used their cultural knowledge to work on literacy. Volunteers had strategies to work with different backgrounds around something in common for us all—literacy.

Relationships With the Media

In the current political climate where education is everyone's top priority, particularly around election time, it is important to maintain a presence with the media. Journalists and TV media will call on schools routinely to get sound bytes. If the district is large enough to have a communications person, the requests often come to that office and are addressed there. However, it is often the case that journalists or

TV reporters will call on leaders to respond to a query. It is important to use the opportunity to educate and spread the good news.

Principal organizations such as National Association of Secondary School Principals (NASSP) have publications about how to deal successfully with the media (http://nasspcms.principals.org/s_nassp/bin.asp).

Paul Young (2004) also suggests some key points:

• It is important to be prepared for a media event. Practice dealing with them in case of a crisis. They will call on you, usually in the case of a tragedy, and will expect you to say something profound.

• Designate a spokesperson for the district or building. Prepare this person on how to answer certain questions. For example, in training for a lock-down, heaven forbid, in case of an intruder, local police and the school district spokesperson designate a spot for media and then will give them times to meet where the police and school will give updates. By assigning a location and times, it helps keep the media from being intrusive physically and emotionally. It is important to get the message you desire to the media so they do not create their own interpretation.

• Sometimes a reporter calls for an interpretation of a recent political action. Use the statements prepared by professional organizations as starting points.

• Train your secretary as to your expectations. If a reporter calls, the secretary can tell the reporter that you will call back within a half hour or so, therefore, giving you time to prepare an intelligent response. It is not necessary to take their calls immediately. They do like to catch people unaware so they can get newsy sound bytes. However, their goal and yours may not be the same. You get to decide how to handle it (pp. 115–116).

Role of Public Relations

Dealing with the media is only one aspect of creating positive public relations. The administrator is only one person; the role of creating positive public relations can be shared with many people, students, and community alike.

Michael Carr, author of "Getting Your School Community to Help with Public Relations" published in *NASSP NewsLeader* in November of 2003, suggests that in the business world, customers are often spokespeople for the products and services provided. One thing he suggests is to create a public relations advisory board. This could even be a subcommittee of the site council with the task of sharing good news about the school. Carr also talks about celebrating good news. We all know how important that is. He suggests annual get-togethers that honor progress, outstanding students, staff members, and volunteers.

Working on positive public relations is important in working with the media. It is important to send positive news releases to local newspapers, radio, and television stations. However, it is frustrating because it is much more difficult to get positive news broadcast in the media than it is negative, sensational items.

For example, once our high school was recognized as a Blue Ribbon High School. We had a day of celebration and invited the television stations, newspapers, mayor, and so on. No one showed up. However, if there had been a fight or some tragedy, they all would have been there very quickly.

However, we now have technology so we can publish our own positive news on our Web sites. It is important to have websites that are current and appealing. Many parents will check out the district website, school website, and individual teacher website. It is important to use all of them to spread the good word.

Use local cable television to broadcast the news. Many districts broadcast school board meetings and many other events on the local cable channel. Board meetings can then be used to share information to educate the community. There may be reports about the math curriculum or about the gifted program. Concerts, award ceremonies, and other events can be broadcast throughout a month. One can publish the broadcast schedule on the district website so people can tune in, or record a certain event, at specific times if they wish.

Tech people may even tape certain events for parents so they can purchase them for the cost of their production. Some districts sell copies of graduation, concerts, and awards. This type of service is invaluable to parents in celebrating the good things that happen in the schools.

Another technological tool that helps with public relations is the ability to have a call-out system that is programmed to call all parents in a building, for example, and remind parents about upcoming events, such as conferences or curriculum nights. It can be used to alert parents in case of emergencies, such as school closing. We have used it to remind parents about the upcoming day of testing to make certain that their children get adequate rest on the night before the tests and come prepared to do their very best. Our families have appreciated this brief reminder, and it is one more connection with our community.

Role of Legislatures and Lawmakers

Everyone seems to be an "education governor," "education president," or "education senator" because public education has become increasingly political at the local, state, and national levels. Current federal legislation and the move toward accountability have changed the landscape.

Therefore, it is important for all administrators to be well read as to both sides of issues. It is important to understand the viewpoints of legislators. It is important to converse with them and help educate them. Building relationships with local legislators is also helpful for them because if an issue arises at the legislative level, they, too, have someone to call to gather information. A helpful conduit of information can be created for information to flow back and forth.

For example, a district has a Legislative Action Committee, composed of board member, communications coordinator, the local education association representative, and parents. They develop a platform that is brought to the Board of Education for approval. Then they work with state legislators in the local community and other neighboring communities to build support for the platform. It is important for administrators to be aware of the platform and be able to converse about it if an occasion arises, such as parent meetings, site councils, and so on.

It is important to communicate to lawmakers about issues that are important. It is amazing the weight of a letter to a legislator. They believe that if someone takes the time to write, then there are many others out there with the same opinion. Some legislators pay more attention to letters than to blanket emails. It is important to know if that is the case.

Other legislators pay special attention to letters from parents, in particular, as opposed to letters from educators. Therefore, if there is an issue that is important to the district, talk to the site council about getting parents to write letters to the legislators. For example, if the issue is about funding the basic formula for schools and parents feel strongly that the formula should be increased, give a list of the legislators' names and addresses to the site councils and ask that they distribute them to parents to write letters.

It is important to provide data, not just emotions, to legislators. Use communication as a tool to educate and shape their opinion. Just because everyone has been through school, does not mean that there is an understanding of the intricacies and difficulties of our job. Invite the legislators to a building for a visit. Besides, they like the photo opportunity, and the school can use it as an opportunity to relay a message.

Role of Law Enforcement

Many schools and school districts employ police liaison officers and/or DARE officers. The symbiotic relationship is invaluable to an administrator. Liaison officers are often a special type of police officer. Frequently the officer that requests this assignment is someone interested in intervening in the lives of young people before offenses and consequences become more serious. Because liaison officers are paid partly from district coffers, they are considered district employees, which entitles them to the rights of district employees in the need-to-know for data. A liaison officer can look in a student's cumulative folder while a regular police officer has certain prohibitions. A liaison officer can be part of investigations because school officials can operate from the basis of "reasonable suspicion" whereas police officers are bound by "probable cause." This seamless intervention with law enforcement facilitates working through some difficult problems in a manner that is more supportive to students and families.

For example, a student is found with contraband. The liaison officer is on campus and can work with the assistant principal or principal as they work through the school process. They can meet with parents in the school setting, which is less fearful than a police station. Particularly if it is a first offense, the officer can explain the consequences and help educate the student and his or her parents with the hopes that it never happens again.

Drug dogs come to the high school several times a year. In working with the police department, we hoped to set a tone for the school and the community that drugs were unhealthy and were not allowed. We had educational seminars in our homerooms as well so that we approached the problem from an educational and enforcement viewpoint. In addition, we held parent meetings with the liaison officer and the principal as chair people in order to address what they were seeing in the community and to ask for parent help. Parents began to establish parent networks where they agreed to host drug-free parties in their home, for example.

Working closely with the police department is just one more connection with the community.

Role of Churches

In many communities churches provide opportunities for students to volunteer and give back to the community. Church groups often contact the schools because they have retired citizens or young people who want to volunteer. It is important for the principal to know the ministers, priests, rabbis, or imams of the local organizations.

In small communities it is not uncommon for banquets to be held in church facilities because they are the only facilities capable of hosting large groups. It is important to utilize such relationships.

It is important to network but also to remember the laws regarding the separation of church and state. Legal seminars constantly deal with current issues as they arise, such as prayer at graduation, prayer at the flagpole, and use of school facilities by church groups. Schools and churches are both institutions that have a great deal of influence on shaping the type of students and communities that we live in. It is important to share the work within the parameters of the law.

Summary

It is the job of every person in the school system to build relationships with parents and the community. It is the task of the administrator(s) to set the -appropriate tone. Still, the most important relationships we can build are with the students in our building by providing a positive climate and a powerful learning experience.

Next, it is our task to reach out and connect with parents and other organizations within a community. Although the phrase "it takes a village to raise a child" is shopworn, it is still true. As the physical boundaries of countries in the world become less distinct because of multinational companies and technology that spans the globe regardless of time zones, the world seems closer yet so far away. It becomes increasingly important to provide an anchor, a touchstone, and a center for our communities. In most communities, that is the school.

Robert Fulghum, in his book *All I Really Need to Know I Learned in Kindergarten: Uncommon Thoughts on Common Things* (1988), said it well: "and it is still true, no matter how old you are—when you go out into the world, it is best to hold hands and stick together" (p. 8).

Personal Journal

1. What are things I do to connect with parents?

2. How do I build community connections?

3. What ideas did I get from this chapter that I can incorporate?

Group Discussion

1. Look at the ways that the building communicates with parents. What are some ways to enhance the communications and networks with the greater community?

2. Look at the building from an outsider's perspective. What is the first thing a visitor sees? What type of message does that give the community? What is visible in the halls? What is the message the community gets when coming to the building?

6

"No, Virginia, There Is No Magic Bullet Curriculum"

The use of the word *curriculum* is bandied about as though everyone knows what it is and where to find it. People look for the right one, a new one, or one that will close the achievement gap. Some people believe that if only they had a "magic bullet" curriculum, the right reading series or the latest program developed on "brain-based learning" (all learning is brain-based, by the way), then the achievement gap would disappear. However, curriculum is not just a textbook, or a series of books. In reality, it is a complex blend and interaction of content, process, and intuition.

Parents call the curriculum office asking for a "copy" of the curriculum so they can compare districts or make certain their child is ready for the next grade. To them, that means they are asking for a copy of the textbook or a list of five or six major concepts that are covered in each subject area by the end of the year.

Such ideas are naïve and represent the lack of common knowledge and vocabulary around the concept of curriculum. A curriculum is so much more than a textbook. In addition to the "stuff" of what we teach, curriculum is also the "how." Materials, such as a textbook, are only tools in a process of interaction among teachers and students in how to create learning. Learning is more than just knowing answers to *Trivial Pursuit* questions and ACT questions. It is the process of how we understand the conflict in the Middle East, how we understand the electoral college, or how we use mathematics to calculate the height of the Golden Gate Bridge.

That's why curriculum is also part intuition. A teacher takes content, uses process, and differentiates to differing learners and learning styles and combines them in a manner that is part intuition, part skill, part training, part luck, and part metacognition.

It is an astonishing fact that curriculum and its development are omitted from some administrative training programs. But it is even more alarming that it is omitted from teacher-training programs. For example, at one university the text for the educational psychology course is *Educational Psychology: Windows on Classrooms* (2004) by Paul Eggen and Don Kauchak. Within this text are chapters on the development of language, social skills, and learner differences. The student learns about learning theory and classroom processes and about student assessment through classroom learning and standardized testing. However, there is no chapter or discussion on how curriculum is developed, monitored, or examined or even what constitutes a good curriculum.

It will be the task of an educated instructional leader to understand curriculum, its development, implementation, and interaction with assessment, accountability, and professional development.

What is good curriculum? What is a scope and sequence? How do we embed state and national standards into the curriculum? What does "research-based" mean? What is "best practice"? How do we best integrate technology into curriculum? What is the role of assessment in curriculum adoption? How do we develop cultural proficiency by choosing good curricula? Who is responsible for any or all of the above topics? What is the administrator's role in this development?

Each of those topics is the subject of many books, but the goal of this book is to provide a basic conceptual knowledge of the topics. In addition, this text will suggest resources for further study.

Terms

There are a few terms that everyone must understand.

1. Curriculum. One of the best resources for administrators is the book published by the Association for Supervision and Curriculum Development (ASCD) called *Planning and Organizing for Curriculum Renewal* updated in 2004. Revised periodically to keep the document fresh, it provides an overview for administrators and teacher-leaders alike when pursuing more information about curriculum development.

ASCD defines curriculum as a "system for guiding and facilitating student learning with the context of consensus-driven accountability standards and organizational productivity targets" (p. 1). It is more than "written products such as scope and sequence documents. . . . It encompasses . . . a much more comprehensive range of processes that begin with stakeholders' shared ideas about the purpose and outcomes of education reframed as long-range goals and measurable objectives, commonly referred to as 'standards' during this time of high stakes accountability" (p. 1).

In layman's language, curriculum is a combination of what we teach, how we teach it, how we know it is learned, and how we modify it to meet the needs of different learners. Curriculum does not equate to the series of textbooks that were adopted. If it were possible to have the perfect curriculum so that all students would learn, textbook companies would go out of business. No one book, no one teacher, no one delivery system will work for all learners all the time. Instead, curriculum is a combination of the tools we use to discover information such as the processes by which learning occurs and the reteaching and differentiation of learning.

A caveat: Too often we use the idea to describe what is "covered" in a classroom. It is important to remember that "coverage" is a teacher term (i.e., how much is covered; how much more has to be covered before the end of the year or semester; etc.). In contrast, *learning* is a student term. What is learned is what is important. Putting the idea of curriculum into student terms changes the focus from adult to student, which is where it should be. Therefore, it is important to remember that curriculum must be considered from a student's point of view—what and how something is learned, not what is "covered."

We know from research that students learn more if important topics are covered in depth, rather than many topics "covered" quickly and briefly. Rather than "an inch deep and a mile wide," teachers need to use curriculum to go "a mile deep and an inch wide."

Therefore, a good curriculum is one that is designed to provide learning opportunities in a rich manner that allows students to probe deeply into content areas, one that allows for diversity of opinions, one that allows students to learn in a manner that the knowledge is retained and is used to gather new knowledge in a spiraling manner.

2. Articulated curriculum. A strong, articulated curriculum has been proven to lead to academic achievement. A good curriculum is "articulated" across all grade levels, meaning that the concepts are planned so that ideas are introduced, expanded, and then used to grasp other knowledge in a developmentally appropriate manner. An infant first learns to babble, then realizes that the "ma ma ma" sound grabs the attention of this wonderful being called mom, and then later that that powerful word *mom* can be used deliberately to get attention, food, love, and laughs.

In school, for example, what is introduced in third grade is built upon in seventh and then used to learn new skills in high school. For example, math facts are introduced in elementary school; the facts are used to solve simple problems in middle school; and in high school those facts are hidden in the complex system of mathematics to be used to solve complex calculus problems.

In a well-articulated curriculum, it is important to plan where ideas are introduced, where they are rehearsed, and where they are used to gather more complex information. Articulation considers what is age-appropriate for students.

Articulation demands that teachers look for places where material is covered over and over without expanding the conceptual base. It is important to consider Bloom's taxonomy in this process.

The process of articulation often discovers that there are topics that are covered in more than one grade level, where concepts are reintroduced, or overlap, several times without advancing the study. In addition, sometimes articulation processes discover what I call "underlapping," key ideas that have been omitted. For example, in American history, one "underlap" we discovered was that students never got past the study of the Vietnam War. Students never studied what has happened in the last 40 years. Students missed the fall of the Berlin Wall, information on multinationalization, and many other key concepts that lead to an understanding of current events.

Articulation also demands that curriculum align with local, state, and national standards. In this time of accountability, it is assumed that the local standards and benchmarks will be covered so that when students are assessed, they will be able to demonstrate knowledge in a manner that shows the school and district are demonstrating Adequate Yearly Progress (AYP).

It is important to remember that state standards are *basics*, which all students must know. Those standards are not high standards. It is important that as curricula are articulated, that differentiated activities and knowledge are delineated for those students who go beyond the basics so that we expect students to provide a rich learning experience.

3. Scope and sequence. A scope and sequence is the scope of what is to be taught and the sequence in which that is done. Scope and sequence documents are what curriculum committees used to write, put in three ring binders, and put on a shelf. Scope and sequence are "articulated" in spiraling fashion levels so that teachers know exactly what must be taught and at what developmentally appropriate level. For example, the idea of topic sentence is introduced in third grade. In seventh grade the student must write a three-paragraph paper, and it is assumed that topic sentences will be in each paragraph. By the senior year research paper, teachers are aware of topic sentences but are more interested in how ideas are developed, how supporting details are used and documented to support those topic ideas.

Many publishing companies provide scope and sequence documents as accompaniments to their textbook series. However, an individual district may want to adapt the documents to the needs of the particular school and district. In most places scope and sequence work has been replaced by work in aligning curriculum to state standards because that is what will be assessed.

Those old scope and sequence documents are still comforting to many people. The process to develop them was important to those on the committee, but the documents had a way of being dusted off and examined, rewritten, and then put back on the shelf.

The process of development itself was a powerful professional development to those on the committee, but because of the way schools are organized, it is difficult to get this information dispersed to all involved staff members. So the documents were a visible product of a curriculum review process, but they were not used effectively in many situations. It is as my son once said as he described some camping stools that did not work very well, "They are nice to have but not nice to use."

With electronic repositories and state standards, the review process is more immediate and more alive. Information may be housed electronically and can be updated on a regular basis. The scope and sequence is readily available to all and can be updated as needed. However, some teachers sometimes feel less comfortable without hard copies, and will print out the information anyway. It is important as an educational leader to help people move beyond that.

The management piece for an educational leader is that the leader must be conversant with any electronic repositories and must be aware of what the teachers are responsible to teach. The leader must be aware of the grade level standards that apply to the level of building. The leader needs to know what to expect in a classroom and how to communicate that to parents.

4. **Essential questions.** Essential questions define the key learnings, the "enduring understandings" as Jay McTighe and Grant Wiggins,

authors of *Understanding by Design* (2004), have described. Essential questions determine the big picture, what a teacher believes a student must know when finished with a unit or chapter or year of study. These are the concepts that are in a teacher's mind when they design instruction. The essential questions align with state standards to shape what it is that a student must know.

"An essential question is the heart of the curriculum. It is the essence of what you believe students should examine and know in the short time they have with you" (Jacobs, 1997, p. 26). It is the WHY of "why do I have to learn this?" Before planning any unit or thinking about a school year, a teacher consciously or unconsciously plans what it is students need to know by the time they have completed their work with that teacher. It is not crucial that students know the main character of *To Kill a Mockingbird*; what is important is for students to understand character development within a novel and how themes emerge in literature. Characters give us insight into the human condition. Essential learnings that answer essential questions are not the "stuff" of *Trivial Pursuit* or *Jeopardy*. They are the "stuff" of life.

For instance, an example for a middle school band essential question for the year is, "How is music a universal language?" Then, as the band teacher designs individual instruction to gain expertise on an instrument, the instructor chooses developmentally appropriate music from many cultures and discusses each with students as they learn to play the music.

The essential question cannot be tested by a simple multiple-choice question but must be developed, explained, and put in context. For example, an example of an essential question for writing is, "What am I trying to achieve with my writing?" The skills needed underneath are knowledge of the audience—who is the paper for—and what is the purpose of the paper—to inform? Entertain? Persuade? (McTighe & Wiggins, 2004, p. 120).

An essential question is NOT "What were three causes of the Civil War?" That question can be answered by filling in three blanks. However, teaching about the Civil War is deeper. It is about the conflict of economies, philosophies, and lifestyles. Therefore, one of the essential questions about the war could be "How did differing economic structures lead to a divided country?"

Teachers have asked how essential questions are different from learning objectives. Although relatively subtle, the difference is crucial. Learning objectives are finite objects that can be assessed by multiple-choice questions. Essential questions define the essence of why a student must learn something. A learning objective may be to be able to use a quadratic equation. An essential question is, "When is a quadratic equation used in real life?"

Using questions forces teachers to think about the purpose for teaching what they are teaching. On curriculum committees it has been difficult for teachers to reshape their thinking in this fashion but once they understand the nature of the "bigness" of the questions, that this is unconsciously how they teach, how they need to put those good thoughts on paper, it becomes a liberating idea. Then teachers are able to prioritize, eliminate nonessential information from "coverage" in texts, and focus their teaching to provide connections for students.

For example, years ago, I sat with a co-worker of mine to help design a biology course for "divergent" learners, meaning these students could not just recite the vocabulary from the textbook-heavy course. We were designing the essential curriculum of key concepts for our students. I asked him to think about each chapter and what three things were in each chapter that he wanted students to know by the end of the unit.

For example, when we were on photosynthesis and respiration, he wanted them to understand that photosynthesis and respiration were reciprocal processes, that both are necessary for continued life on this planet. It was important to know the key ingredients for making those processes happen so that students understood the relationship with pollution and air quality. To memorize the exact formula was not necessary, but it was important to understand the interplay of plants and animals, that plants give us oxygen, and that trees clean carbon dioxide from the air and are used in some cities to clean up the air pollution. It was important to understand that sugars are a by-product, which leads ultimately to food for animals.

Therefore, we planned each lesson with the three essential questions that each student would answer by the end of that chapter. We began each unit by sharing the essential questions with students.

The students also knew that those essential questions would define the assessments at the end of the units. For photosynthesis, they had to be able to talk about respiration as the opposite process and to discuss why that was important. They had to be able to define how sugars were a by-product and why that was important to humans.

We did this before the term *essential questions* was coined.

An important way to use essential questions is for teachers to post them in their classroom at the beginning of the unit. Students understand the direction and focus of their learning. This particularly helps the student who is a whole-to-part learner because it provides a framework for his learning. It provides the "coat rack" where a student can hang his information. It helps students know what they will be responsible for in an assessment because assessments should be a natural outgrowth of instruction and not a surprise. Assessments should be a synthesis of the written, taught, and learned curriculum.

Therefore, curriculum design, in going from big picture to specifics, is as follows:

- Essential questions for year
- Essential questions for unit—the most important
- Skills/content that students must know/do to answer the essential questions
- Standards—state and national that must be addressed
- Assessments—how are the essential questions being assessed? Hopefully, the standards assessments and teacher assessments are the same.

5. Standards. In our time of accountability each state has developed standards that students must know. The standards are the *basics* upon which higher knowledge is built. Schools are assessed against the achievement of these standards for their statewide reporting system that is currently mandated by federal law.

Some states have written their standards in bands—across grade levels—and others have grade-level standards. For example, science standards may be banded across grades 3–5, 6–8, and high school, while social studies could be described by what students must know at each grade level. How a state defines the standards also defines how they are assessed.

Banded standards allow individual districts more latitude as to when material is taught. The district must then place them in a fashion that is developmentally appropriate. There is less flexibility if the standards are specific to grade level. Either way, a district must match when the material of the standards is taught and when they are assessed.

Each state must then develop tests based on the standards. The results of these tests are then reported to the public so that parents and community can make a determination as to the academic progress of students within a school and district and how that compares to other districts in the state. The academic progress—or not—is what is defined currently as AYP. There is more on the accountability system in a later chapter.

6. Mapping. Mapping is a term used by Heidi Hayes Jacobs, adjunct associate professor of the Department of Curriculum and Teaching at Teachers College, Columbia University and author of *Mapping the Big Picture* (1997) and other books, to describe a process where curriculum is charted in a visual format. Mapping lays out "process and skills emphasized, the content in terms of essential concepts and topics, and products and performances that are the assessments of learning" (p. 8).

We also use mapping to design differentiated instruction. We design learning that will allow some students to go deeper and, provide opportunities for others to have avenues for relearning, if the concepts were not mastered.

Mapping is a process curriculum committees use to get a visual representation of what is taught in which grades. It facilitates articulation in that it allows everyone to see the curriculum K–12. Jacobs feels it is "crucial that each teacher complete a calendar based map" (1997, p.8). The purpose of maps for her is to collect data on what is taught.

Maps can be done in several ways. They can be by month, by topic area, or by strand for academic standards. It is important to find what works best in your district and use it. Jacobs talks about using a monthly map, which works better for elementary people as opposed to secondary. It is more helpful for secondary teachers to map by strand, such as expository writing, from grades six through eight. Then teachers can see what foundations are laid at an early age, can assume that students have certain skills, and can build from there.

In the mapping process, teachers of like grades or subject areas write on big chart paper—some people are using technological mapping tools—**to write down exactly what is taught**. It is important to have more than one representative per grade level, particularly if there are several buildings in the district because teachers have a tendency to teach what they want behind closed doors whether or not that matches the written curriculum of the district. The maps are often a surprise because not all sixth-grade teachers, for example, teach the same thing. If that is true, then different buildings need to each do their own maps so the larger team can discuss this.

Part of the mapping process is to have teachers write down how the learning is assessed. The mapping can be done on T charts so that the material is on one side and the assessments on the other. It is important to stress the correlation of curriculum and assessment.

- PreK–12 grade-level teams need to **look at the big picture** across grade levels to see: What is the taught curriculum? What is missing? What is repeated? What are overlaps? And what I call "underlaps"? What's not there?
- Is the instruction spiraling so that material is introduced, reinforced, and then used as a foundation for more advanced study? Or is the material repeatedly introduced and the instruction always at low levels in Bloom's taxonomy?

- How is material assessed? Do the assessments match what is taught?
- Are state and national standards embedded? Do they match the local assessments?
- Are the timelines appropriate?

In working through the process, it is sometimes difficult for teachers to give up pet units. However, by using essential questions and the articulation process, teachers can see how the entire curriculum builds upon itself to create a strong developmental sequence.

7. Assessment. The words *assessment* and *tests* are not interchangeable. The purpose of assessment should be to guide instruction. The purpose of tests has too often been to "give" grades or use as a sorting tool—those who "got it" and those who did not.

However, the whole accountability atmosphere has helped us understand that valid assessment helps us understand what a student knows or not. Then it is the task of the teacher to make certain that key concepts are learned because that is what will be assessed on state tests.

We have formative assessment and summative assessment. Formative assessment helps us understand what a student does or does not know and then how to shape instruction so that the learning occurs. Teachers use formal and informal strategies to shape instruction. They may use oral questioning techniques to get a feeling of what students know. Or some teachers ask a key question from the day's lesson and have students write their answer on a card, called an "exit card" because then the cards are handed in at the end of the hour. The teacher can then see how well the concept is understood as the next day's lesson is planned. If everyone understands, then the group can move forward. If, however, there is a lack of understanding, then the teacher plans reteaching for some or the entire group.

Summative assessment is the assessment at the end of learning so that we understand how much has been learned. We have concentrated on summative assessment in the past, and thankfully, we are recognizing the value of formative assessment.

Good teachers are constantly assessing, formally and informally, what students are learning. They walk around the room to see where students are struggling, they ask more questions of a student to help shape thinking, and they ask students to show them. Assessments are not just paper-and-pencil tests but also an integral part of shaping the curriculum.

Assessments need to be a direct outgrowth of the essential questions. Wiggins and McTighe (2004) believe that "the performance tasks and related sources of evidence—are designed *prior* to the lessons," which is part of "backward design" (p. 17). In curriculum design, it is powerful to have teachers discover their essential questions, design the final assessment, and then discover the skills and content students need to learn in order to master the assessment.

Developing common assessments for common courses is a powerful tool to improve student achievement and create a meaningful professional learning community. The assessments can then be used to see how well students do in certain areas. One teacher's students may have done better on paragraph structure than another teacher's. This can be discussed at a team meeting in a nonthreatening atmosphere of trust. Teachers can ask, "What did you do?" I did . . . but it didn't seem to work as well as I hoped. How did you do it?"

In their book on *Professional Learning Communities at Work* (1998), DuFour and Eaker stated "professional teachers focus on performance and production" (p. 218) and they "routinely collaborate with their colleagues" (p. 219). Using the common assessments as a focal point allows teachers to improve their practice by using hands-on topics. Such a discussion among teachers may also stimulate the awareness that there is a need for professional development and training in a certain area. Meaningful professional development is job-embedded, meaning that teachers engage in a process that is "engaged in the ongoing cycle of inquiry, reflection, dialogues, action, analysis, and adjustments in order to improve results and give one another feedback as they practice new skills" (DuFour & Eaker, 1998, p. 273). The administrator can then be a resource to provide time, money, or appropriate training to meet the needs of a team or individual.

Different Types of Curricula

There are different types of curricula as described by ASCD, which are as follows:

1. **Recommended**—that content recommended by experts in the field containing standards of what students should know in this area. These curricula have little impact on written curricula and little effect on classroom teachers.

2. **Written**—that which is found in documents prepared by the state, the school, and/or the teacher containing a scope and sequence. There is a moderate influence on taught curriculum.

FCRR

Benchmarks (4A's TPRI)

3. **Supported**—the one for which instructional materials are available—software, textbooks. This one has strong influence on taught curriculum.

4. **Tested**—that which is actually assessed by state, school, or teacher. This is the strongest influence on what is actually taught.

5. **Taught**—that which is actually delivered in classrooms.

6. **Learned**—the "bottom line" that students learn. THE MOST IMPORTANT OF ALL. There is often a significant gap between taught and learned curricula.

7. **Hidden**—the unintended curriculum, which may or may not be funded or prioritized. For example, reading is taught for 120 minutes a day while art is taught for 30 minutes every other day. Therefore, one can interpret that art does not matter as much as reading.

8. **Excluded**—that which is omitted. The importance of African Americans, women, etc. in our history is an example of that which has been excluded. Hidden and excluded curricula have strong influence on students' perceptions. (ASCD, pp. 1–2)

What Is a Good Curriculum?

A **good curriculum**, according to ASCD, has several guidelines:

1. Students and teachers are able to **study important topics and skills in depth.** Curriculum topics should be a "mile deep and an inch wide." Too often teachers get hung up on the idea of coverage, as described above. Therefore, it is important to establish the essential learnings that students need to know and then use resources, such as textbooks, as tools to make that happen. It is not necessary to start in the beginning of a book and progress page by page to the end to make certain that "we get it all in."

It is seductive to equate the textbook with THE curriculum. Textbook companies would like that. However, it is important to realize that book companies are big corporations and getting bigger all the time and that they have a product to sell. Book companies compete for adoptions particularly from states such as Texas and California who do statewide adoptions. Textbook companies write their materials so that they appeal to as many groups as possible, committing the same fallacy about coverage.

It is important, therefore, to establish what it is that your students need to know, establish the essential questions that match standards, and then pick materials.

2. Students should use **various learning strategies to solve problems**. Students should be able to build learning within a context of complex meaningful problems.

One curriculum controversy is about integrated or reform math approaches versus traditional. In the integrated math, students are allowed to explore more than one right way to solve a problem. Research shows that students in this approach do better on problem solving on standardized tests. Plus, their math achievement stays high. In years past, American students did not do as well as their Asian counterparts in the area of problem solving. Is it because we were taught only one correct way to do math out of a context of meaningful problems? One wonders . . . Life is complex, and students should reflect the complexity of life in their problem solving in a wide variety of curricular areas.

3. Curricula should teach **both content and process**; it is not an either/or proposition. Students should not concentrate on rote skills at the expense of learning metacognitive strategies about how their learning occurs. One of the greatest gifts any teacher can give a student, regardless of the student's age, is to help him figure out how he solved a problem. Help him understand the thinking process so that he can repeat it. I call that "metateaching." It is about teaching students how to be lifelong learners. They will continue to learn once they leave an individual's classroom and, if students understand how they learned something successfully, they will be able to repeat that and build upon it.

However, if they use a random approach to learning and do not understand why certain strategies worked, they will spend too much time using a hit and miss approach as opposed to having the skill to repeat a successful performance.

4. Curricula should respond to differences in **student learning preferences**. No one mode of presentation should be used exclusively. There is no one right way and no one wrong way. However, young children tend to be hands-on and as children grow, they can learn in more abstract ways. It is important to be developmentally appropriate in how we teach.

5. The curriculum should be organized so that learning builds on itself in multiyear spiraling sequences, meaning the curriculum needs to be **well-articulated preK–12**. When one articulates a curriculum, one must build on what we know about how learning takes place. One,

information or skills are introduced; two, they are practiced or rehearsed; and three, mastery is achieved and that learning can be used to begin again with new information that must be introduced.

6. **Emphasize both the academic and the practical**. Students learn and remember information and processes more when they are linked to applicable life situations. Students like learning what they can use. They, interestingly, think that if it connects to real-life and they "get it," that it must be easy. What they do not realize is that it was "easy" because the student had a foundation that incorporated academics and relevant knowledge. All learning should be easy in that it is relevant and links to prior learning.

7. **Develop integrated curricula,** if appropriate. We do not learn in a vacuum. The most important learnings are those that are connected to other learning. Teachers have long known that students are more likely to practice reading on content that is very interesting. Social studies and science content often provide the content for reading passages because the topics are interesting and students want to learn interesting things. Students learn writing and grammar in the context of writing a meaningful letter to a congressman or in a letter to the editor. Learning grammar in isolation is an esoteric study if done outside the context of what it means and how to use it.

8. Focus on the achievement of **essential learning outcomes**, rather than trying to cover everything. It is important to plan curriculum so that it accomplishes the goals of what students need to know and do. What makes the Declaration of Independence unique? How does literature make our lives richer? The establishment and use of essential questions is crucial to the establishment of meaningful, articulated curricula.

9. The **written, taught, tested, and learned curricula should be the same**. Teachers design the essential questions to describe what students must learn. Authentic assessments are then designed to determine what was learned. The establishment of curriculum is a living process, not a collection of written documents that are contained in three-ring binders that are put on a shelf until the next curriculum review process. It is important to constantly revisit whether the written, taught, tested, and learned curriculum are the same (ASCD, pp. 3–4).

Curriculum Review Process

Curriculum is adopted through a process in most districts that is put on a cycle so that energy and resources can be spread out over time.

Most districts use a process that reviews each curricular area every six to seven years. Within that cycle, different tasks must be accomplished. Following is a sample review cycle:

1. Year one:

    - Self-examination—map what is currently being taught.
    - Are the state and national standards taught? Where are they taught?
    - What is current best practice in this subject area?
    - What are other districts, which are known for their quality outcomes, doing?
    - How are the curricula meeting the district goals?

2. Year two:

    - Define essential questions.
    - Map what should be taught.
    - Suggest possible new courses and deletion of old ones.
    - Purchase materials that match needs.
    - Prepare for dissemination of plan—What professional development is needed for staff? Administrators? How will that be accomplished? Who will be responsible for implementation? How will new teachers be trained?
    - Develop common assessments—Schools with effective professional learning communities use common assessments as tools to improve instruction. Teachers who have common teaching assignments develop common assessments that are built on the essential questions that students need to know. For example, fourth-grade teachers can look at their students' math scores to see how they are doing. All ninth-grade civics teachers can get together to decide what students need to know.
    - Curriculum writing time is provided for teachers for refining previously taught courses and developing new ones.

3. Year three through six (seven)

    - Implement and make minor adjustments as people work through the curriculum. Supplemental materials may need to be added and assessments refined.
    - Monitor academic progress for national requirement of the No Child Left Behind Act (NCLB) and make adjustments if necessary.
    - Refine common assessment.

Implementation and Professional Development

Curriculum adoption is just the beginning of a process. Adoption is not successful unless there is a successful implementation. Unfortunately, the follow-through on implementation has been the weak spot in most review cycles. Teachers on curriculum committees often ask, "Who will be responsible to make certain the curriculum is implemented in the classroom?" The answer is that it is the administrator's responsibility—this is a management and instructional leader's responsibility—but this is difficult because of the way schools are structured. It is so easy for teachers to close their doors and teach what they want without much scrutiny. It is impossible for an administrator to be in every classroom every day and every minute of the day. In addition, there are so many tasks that demand immediate attention that this task is not always in the forefront of an administrator's mind. It is assumed that after the review process with that intense work that teachers will follow through and implement. But that does not always happen. The key to successful implementation is to keep the curriculum process alive and in the state of constant examination.

Technology is helping because there are electronic databases that can replace the three-ring binders. There are e-curriculum databases that contain the information so it is accessible through a staff Intranet, without the paper gathering dust on a shelf. Teachers can print it out if necessary. The electronic nature makes the curriculum more visible to all teachers. Plus, it allows the curriculum to be modified easily without reprinting a major document. On professional development days, teachers can examine their essential questions, the skills/contents, and the assessments to make certain they are relevant and successful. Concepts can be changed and updated easily to meet current needs.

In this current time of accountability, successful implementation is more visible and necessary. It will become increasingly apparent what skills students have and what they are lacking and which teachers are successful or not at teaching those skills.

Districts are purchasing data drill-down software that allows access to the hard data of what students know, what they do not know, and what teachers are most successful in teaching. We will be able to pull up a list of students and see if they have certain skills and we will be able to see at what grade level they earned them and what teacher they had. Although this is intimidating to some teachers, it is important to create an atmosphere that is not competitive among teachers. It is important for administrators to be able to know where the curriculum is being taught and where students are mastering the content. Again, this becomes a management task for the educational leader.

It is important for administrators to sit on curriculum committees as various areas come up for review. One way for administrators to grow professionally is for them to volunteer to be on a committee outside of their own area of study. Each curricular area has its unique issues. An administrator gains a richer understanding of that area if he or she can sit on a committee as teachers shape essential questions and assessments. Because administrators have a big-picture framework of the organization, they can offer insights that can help the committees think outside of their own specific area. Being aware of the unique personality of each area helps the administrator build a better schedule and supervise staff in a more effective manner, which marries the work of a manager and educational leader.

State and National Standards

What role do state and national standards play in adopting a good curriculum? States develop their own standards and national organizations do likewise. In *Content Knowledge: A Compendium of Standards and Benchmarks for K–12 Education* (1997), John Kendall and Robert Marzano compiled standards from various organizations to give a composite, which is very helpful as districts look to best practice as they review and adopt curricula.

State standards are important guideposts as the federal law of NCLB assesses how students do or do not make AYP. It is important to make certain that the standards are addressed in the district curriculum. The standards are what will be assessed and made public as an accounting of progress by the school.

However, it is important to remember that state standards are the minimum of what students must know. It is crucial for teams to build from there and have high expectations for students.

The Role of Leaders and Managers

Instructional leaders have four major roles in the curriculum process.

1. **Understand the process.** Districts may have curriculum directors or teachers on special assignment that devote their energies to this

process. However, in some districts, the principal and assistant principal do it all. It is important for administrators to understand the process regardless of who is in charge. It is helpful for principals to be an active part of curriculum review committees because they bring a global perspective that teachers and parents may not have.

2. **Oversee the process.** If the principal has teacher-leaders or a curriculum director on staff, then the principal can be a part of the process. If they are in charge, then they will have to guide the process of mapping, designing essential questions, choosing materials, providing professional development, and monitoring implementation.

3. **Monitor implementation.** Teachers always ask who is responsible for making certain that all teachers are teaching the district's curriculum. Professionally, it is the responsibility of each teacher to do this. However, it is the principal's job to make certain it is happening. Being part of a curriculum committee is helpful in the implementation because then the principal knows the discussion that went into the process.

4. **Act as liaison with parents and the community to be able to describe the curriculum.** When administrators understand what is being taught and why, they are able to answer questions successfully from parents and community. They are able to be a liaison from classroom to community.

Summary

A strong, well-articulated preK–12 curriculum is key to student achievement. The curriculum must address the state standards because that is what will be assessed and reported to the public to see if the school is making its AYP. Curriculum, standards, assessment, accountability, and job-embedded professional development are intertwined in a manner that demands that administrators pay attention to what is taught, how it is assessed, how well are students learning, and what professional development needs are present for administrators and teachers.

An instructional leader understands the process, what is taught, how it is taught and is able to convey that message to students, parents, and community. The leader monitors the successful implementation of the curriculum and is able to plan for meaningful professional development as needed to implement the curriculum.

Langston B. Hughes wrote a poem "Theme for English B" which starts:

> The instructor said,
> Go home and write
> A page tonight.
> And let that page come out of you—
> Then, it will be true.
> I wonder if it's that simple? (Chapman, 1968, p. 429)

Curriculum, assessment, and professional development are not that simple. They are complex and need a lot of attention from an educational leader.

Personal Journal

1. What are my strengths as a curriculum leader?

2. How does articulation get accomplished in my school? In my district?

3. What are areas that need to be developed?

Group Discussion

1. How do educational leadership and management work together to create an articulated curriculum that matches standards, assessments, and professional development?

2. In my district who has responsibility for the development and sharing of curriculum? What is my role as educational leader in this process?

7

Focus on Professional Development

Professional development is a fundamental piece of the jigsaw puzzle of curriculum, assessment of student performance, data collection, and improving instructional practices. The ultimate goal of all of the above is student achievement. We as educators are never done learning. This zest for continued growth in knowledge and skill is the energy that fuels a true educational leader whether that person is an administrator or teacher. We are works of art in progress.

In the past, schools have been criticized for days when students are not in school. Community members ask, "What do teachers do on all of those days off?" Community members may not understand the professional development that occurs on those days.

Prior to the major accountability movement, professional development has been haphazard and individualistic at best. Professional development did not necessarily focus on district, site, or learning goals.

Dennis Sparks, executive director of National Staff Development Council, stated, "... it is imperative for professional development to shape leadership and teaching practices that are intended to improve student learning" (Killion, 2002b, foreword). "For various reasons educational leaders might select staff development content and processes that are far too weak to produce the desired results. Instead of being tough-minded in assessing the strength of each link in the causal chain that leads to the intended outcome, leaders often initiate activities that keep everyone busy but are not likely to change much of anything. And then, for various other reasons, leaders overload teachers with too many "projects" directed at too many goals with too many activities. No one could legitimately expect anyone with such a fragmented agenda to implement even *some* of the new practices much less *all* (Killion, 2002b, foreword).

The National Staff Development Council (NSDC) understands that there is a strong correlation between effective professional development and increased student achievement. Through using data in relation to the curriculum, educators develop a rich understanding of what students need and what training educators need to deliver that learning. Then professional development is structured to fill that need. The interplay of all of the items creates a professional learning community where conversations and training revolve around specific student achievement issues.

Putting all the pieces together—curriculum, professional development, assessment, and so on—in a manner that reflects data-driven leadership, the leader can create a professional learning community. By managing the pieces, a leader can create a synergy that creates a culture where the vision of student achievement is embraced by all parties.

In *Professional Learning Community at Work: Best Practices for Enhancing Student Achievement* (1998), DuFour and Eaker described several attributes of a professional learning community: When a school community is focused on the common goal of increased student achievement, then data collection, curriculum, and professional development are focused toward that end. The creation of a professional learning community is the logical outgrowth of providing target professional development to the needs of teachers, in a manner that is described as job-embedded professional development.

Prior to 1994, professional development activities were largely "a disparate set of adult learning activities with few demonstrable results other than participants' mounting frustration" (Mizell, in Roy & Hord, 2003, p. 6). In 1994, National Staff Development Council (NSDC) created a "unique set of materials—staff development standards— which provide a framework for thinking about professional development (Roy & Hord, 2003, p. 6). The standards, which were revised in 2000 so that they would be more effective, "represent a road map to high quality staff development" (Mizell, in Roy & Hord, 2003, p. 6).

An effective school leader needs to use the 12 standards from NSDC as they plan professional development activities. NSDC is an invaluable resource in structuring activities and practices that are rooted in best practice (see www.**nsdc**.org).

Effective Professional Development

Professional Development Standards

It is incumbent upon leaders to know the 12 standards as described by NSDC, which are divided into 3 areas: context, process, and content. In recognition that the purpose of professional development is the increase of student achievement, each of the 12 standards begins with the phrase "Staff development improves the learning of all students..." (in the interest of space that phrase was omitted).

Context Standards:

Learning Communities: . . . organizes adults in learning communities whose goals are aligned with those of the school and district.

Leadership: . . . requires skillful school and district leaders who guide continuous instructional improvement.

Resources: . . . requires resources to support adult learning and collaboration.

Process Standards:

Data-Driven: . . . uses disaggregated student data to determine adult learning priorities, monitor progress, and help sustain continuous improvement.

Evaluation: . . . uses multiple sources of information to guide improvement and demonstrate its impact.

Research-based: . . . uses learning strategies appropriate to the intended goal.

Learning: . . . applies knowledge about human learning and change.

Collaboration: . . . provides educators with the knowledge and skills to collaborate.

Content Standards:

Equity: . . . prepares educators to understand and appreciate all students, create safe, orderly, and supportive learning environments, and hold high expectations for their academic achievement.

Quality Teaching: . . . deepens educators' content knowledge, provides them with research-based instructional strategies to assist students in meeting rigorous academic standards, and prepares them to use various types of classroom assessments appropriately.

Family Involvement: . . . provides educators with knowledge and skills to involve families and other stakeholders appropriately (Killion, 2002b, p. 1).

It is important to know these standards because, when planning training sessions, leaders need to measure the activities against the standards to make certain that the development is of high quality.

Effective Professional Development is NOT

Effective professional development is NOT:

- An isolated event or series of events
- "Sit and get"
- Just to make adults feel good
- Isolated from district and building goals
- An event, rather than a process

Effective Professional Development IS:

Effective professional development has the following *essential* components, according to Joellen Killion, author of *Assessing Impact: Evaluating Staff Development* (2002a):

- Involves the acquisition of research-based knowledge and skill
- Has clear expectations about the implementation of the new learning
- Creates a desire to implement the new learning
- Allows for opportunities to apply the knowledge and to practice the new skills with feedback
- Is grounded in the belief that the practices are valuable
- Has ongoing assessment of the effectiveness of new educator practices by examining student work and reflecting on and refining instructional practice
- Facilitates consistent application of the practices in the classroom
- Utilizes a systemic support for continuous improvement (p. 19)

Therefore, in a nutshell, effective professional development is "job-embedded."

Prior to the accountability movement, and the setting of standards for learning and for professional development, activities have been relatively haphazard and individualized based on personal preference. Some teachers pursued continuous learning and others sat back and did the minimum required to renew the teaching license. Activities were often one- or two-day workshops that may or may not have had direct applicability to the teacher's classroom. This type of professional development may or may not have improved student achievement.

However, with the accountability movement, standards, and student achievement results published in the local newspapers, attention has been focused on the improvement of student achievement. Therefore, there was recognition that effective professional development must be focused on that which "improves the learning of all students" (Killion, 2002b, p. 1). The term *job-embedded* has been used to describe professional development that may be almost surgical in its precision. Teachers need to learn targeted strategies, defined curricula, or a combination of the above.

For example, teams of teachers examine student work. There is a difference in achievement among various classrooms. Then discussion occurs as to why. It may be that certain teachers have certain strategies that other teachers do not have. Then it becomes necessary to provide that training for those teachers in a manner that is directly related to the achievement of specific learning goals.

Or in the math program there are questioning strategies that a teacher needs to use to get students to think about how they solved a problem. Some teachers have not been trained in the strategies and are unable to train the students to think about how they reached solutions. It is necessary to get the teachers this training.

Therefore, the leader helps facilitate job-embedded professional development to increase teacher—and administrative skills—in identified key areas.

Designing Effective Professional Development

To help leaders design effective professional development, Joellen Killion (2002a) provides what she calls "Filtering Questions."

1. Is your staff development program based on NSDC's *Standards for Staff Development, Revised*?

2. Does your staff development program have as its goal both educator learning and student achievement?

3. Is your staff development program sufficiently powerful to produce change in both educator practice and student learning?

4. Do you intend to use the results of this evaluation for ongoing improvement?

5. Do you intend to involve stakeholders in the evaluation?

6. Are you evaluating a staff development program rather than an event? (p. 3)

An example of such an opportunity would be training in using formative assessments. Teachers design common assessments and then spend time discussing student outcomes on those assessments. Those discussions frequently point out the need for certain training that is needed for some teachers or maybe for all.

If, however, someone comes to the administrator to suggest bringing in a speaker on using humor in the classroom, by using the filtering questions, a leader can point out that, although it would be an enjoyable topic, unless the training meets the above characteristics, it is not effective professional development.

Moving Standards Into Practice

It is important to use NSDC standards to establish effective professional development. The next step in creating a total learning community across all stakeholders is to see how those standards affect all stakeholders, not just teachers, to create a districtwide learning community. NSDC has prepared a document entitled *Moving NSDC's Staff Development Standards Into Practice: Innovation Configurations* (2003) by Patricia Roy and Shirley Hord. Roy and Hord developed rubrics, called Innovation Configurations, for each stakeholder group— teachers, principals, central office staff members, superintendents, and school boards—to describe effective practice in each group for the 12 standards.

For each group there are desired outcomes. At the end of the document there is a "Cross Walk" to illustrate the desired outcomes for all role groups. "The idea was to promote systemic responsibility for professional development across all levels of the K–12 system through coherence of the desired outcomes for all role groups" (p. 9).

The rubrics can be used as topics of discussion in many ways. An administrator could use them with teachers, with peers, with an administrative council, or in discussion with a superintendent as part of goal-setting. The instrument could be used as a "broad assessment of a district's or school's program for professional development" (p. 10). Or the document could be used to "reveal the actions" necessary to "develop principals' appropriate knowledge and skills" (p. 10). The maps could be used in a variety of ways because "quality staff development for adults positively impacts students, and the standards clarify what quality staff development is" (p. 10).

By have a conceptual knowledge of the above tools, an instructional leader can use the standards, the filtering questions, and the innovation configurations to shape professional development in a manner that is designed to provide effective growth for staff with improved student achievement as a goal.

The Role of an Instructional Leader

An effective school leader creates a community of learners, students, adults, and parents. To do this a leader needs to:

1. "Lead through shared vision and values rather than through rules and procedures" (DuFour & Eaker, 1998, p. 184). The leader helps define the academic goals by shaping the vision of the school with the vision of the district and the standards that must be met by the state.

2. Be actively involved in the curriculum process, knowing what is taught, how it's assessed, and by gathering data to see how well students are doing. The leader must understand how to gather data, how to ask the right questions, how to dig deep to find "root causes" of issues. Few current administrators have had formal training in this art of data management; we must educate our staffs and ourselves.

3. The administrator must "provide staff with the information, training, and parameters they need to make good decisions" (DuFour & Eaker, 1998, p. 186). The decisions may be around what type of professional development is necessary, what curriculum to use, and what data to gather.

4. The instructional leader must provide support and follow-up to curriculum adoption and professional development activities in a manner that supports the learning of staff and students in a continuous improvement model. Professional learning communities, like job-embedded professional development, are devoted to results (DuFour & Eaker, 1998, p. 261).

5. An instructional leader provides training, time, and resources for reflective practice. Because "we teach who we are," as

described by Parker J. Palmer, author of *The Courage to Teach* (1998), it is important that educators spend time sorting out who that teacher-person is. Professional learning communities create time for reflection, particularly around reflection in professional practice.

Timothy G. Reagan, Charles W. Case, and John W. Brubacher wrote *Becoming a Reflective Educator: How to Build a Culture of Inquiry in the Schools* (2000). Because teaching is a delicate interplay of curriculum, process, and intuition, as described before, it becomes imperative that educators understand who they are. According to Reagan et al., "[the teacher] must engage in *reflection* about his or her practice, just as the physician must reflect about the symptoms and other evidence presented by a patient" (p. 20).

An example of how this can be done is demonstrated by a principal who designed journals for each of her staff, which she gave them at an opening workshop. Each month she published a reflective question that was designed from best practice classroom strategies and expected each teacher to write about it in the journal. At the end of the year when she did final conversations with each staff, she asked them to look at their journals and reflect on key points on their professional practice from the year's journey. Utilizing reflection allows the staff to practice "metateaching," to think about teaching, its implications, and its power.

By creating the professional learning communities, the effective school leader creates a community that is energized, focused, and self-renewing. When the community is focused toward a common goal and energy is devoted to it, teachers get excited, empowered, and creative.

Working With Individual Teachers

Apart from the creation of a learning community as described above as the leader works with the system, an effective school leader must deal with individual teachers within that system to facilitate individual professional development. The system is like a chain in that it is only as strong as its weakest link.

Instructional leaders must work with individual goal-setting conferences as one place to shape professional development and growth, particularly with those teachers who need to move forward. By setting personal goals that are in line with the building's goals and designing professional development that will help that teacher attain those goals, the leader is shaping teachers as individuals who will enhance the whole.

It is important that the leader follows up with the teacher to monitor progress toward reaching the goal. If the teacher shows movement in a positive direction, the leader can develop some sort of recognition—by praise, asking if they want to take a leadership position, or some other such strategy.

If, however, someone continues to resist and is not growing, it may be necessary to do what Jim Collins suggests in *Good to Great* (2001). To move an organization from good to great, he believes it is necessary to get the right people on the bus and, more importantly, get the wrong people off the bus. If teachers are not willing to be professional teachers, it may be time to help them move on.

Working with individuals can be very rewarding to help them design growth opportunities that individuals may not have been aware of. It is rewarding to watch teachers get excited and energized as they grow personally and professionally

Summary

The goal of job-embedded professional development is to improve the learning for students. Effective school leaders create learning environments where students and adults alike are engaged in learning because, if adults are not learning, students are not either. Therefore, it is important that an effective school leader has knowledge of curriculum, assessment practices, and professional development needs. The leader must work with individuals and groups to provide opportunities, time, and money to integrate all of the components in a learning environment. The leader must manage the system to create a reflective community of learners in a manner that engages all stakeholders from teachers to school board members.

Robert Fulghum (1988) described the role of educational leader as a professional developer. "There are those who depend on us, watch us, learn from us, take from us. And we never know. Don't sell yourself short. You may never have proof of your importance, but you are more important than you think" (p. 80).

Personal Journal

1. What was one of the most meaningful professional development opportunities that I have participated in? Why was it so meaningful?

2. What professional development needs have my staff expressed?

3. As I reflect on the comment, "we teach who we are," what does that mean to me?

4. How are professional development activities in my building linked to our goals?

Group Discussion

1. How can the NSDC standards and practices be helpful in developing a professional learning community in our district?

2. How can professional development activities be targeted to those areas that are in the greatest need of assistance? What resources are available? Speakers? Videos? Workshops?

8

What's Special About Special Education

To manage special education, an instructional leader must serve two functions:

First, an administrator must have a SOLID knowledge of special education and law, especially the categories of disabilities, eligibility criteria, and due process. There is a resource for administrators about the facts of special education entitled *What Every Principal Needs to Know About Special Education* (2004) by Margaret J. McLaughlin and Victor Nolet.

Second, a leader must direct the process and be a support to all of those people who interact daily with the intricacies of special education. The process is as important as the factual knowledge. Unfortunately, most of the process skills are gained through experience and trial and error.

Knowledge

It is not enough that only special education directors and teachers know special education. An administrator also must have a solid background in order to serve as a leader in this very intricate, complicated area.

Here is a special education self-test. Can you complete the following acronyms and describe what they mean?

IDEIA

LRE

IEP

ILP

ADA

FAPE

DCD

OHI

LD

EBD

ODD

If you could describe each of the acronyms, hurray. If not, not to worry. Just keep reading.

Just as the federal government passes a law named the Elementary and Secondary Education Act (ESEA, now called No Child Left Behind [NCLB]) every five to seven years to outline its involvement in regular education, it also revisits a federal law about special education. This law is now called the IDEIA of 2004, the Individuals with Disabilities Education Improvement Act. The law has two core requirements:

- A free, appropriate public education, or FAPE, must be provided to all children who have disabilities and are eligible for special education.
- Each child's special education needs must be designed on an individual basis, written into an individual education plan (IEP), and provided in the least restrictive environment (LRE). Just because a child has special education needs does not mean that the child is taught strictly by special education teachers. In fact, that child must still be educated in the mainstream education program as much as possible. Modifications must be determined and made, if necessary.

Special education students are not the sole responsibility of special education teachers. They are still the responsibility of mainstream education with assistance from special education. Each student who has an IEP will have a case manager whose responsibility it is to write the IEP with the help of a team, which consists of administration, regular education teachers, parents, and assessment data. The special education teachers help design the program and then must monitor its implementation, but they are not the only one responsible for its delivery. Depending on the disability and its severity, there may be many others involved in delivering the program. This is difficult for regular education teachers to understand because they too often want special education teachers to be solely responsible for students with special educational needs.

- The rights of every child and the family must be ensured and protected through procedural safeguards called due process. These rights must be shared with parents on a regular basis (McLaughlin & Nolet, 2004, p. 5). It is mandated that parents be involved in setting a child's goals.

Lately, it has been feeling as though parents have become more demanding with individual, specialized requests for their children, but in some ways that is a positive outgrowth of the fact that more parents are becoming better educated about special education and their rights. It is the task of administrators, both building and special education directors, to make certain that the interests of the parents, children, and school maintain an appropriate focus and balance.

There are many categories of children who are in need of special education. We have a tendency to abbreviate the titles for the sake of time, but those ubiquitous acronyms make special education seem as though it has its own unique language. Some of the titles are learning disabled (LD), emotionally/behaviorally disordered or emotionally disordered (E/BD or ED), developmentally cognitively disabled (DCD), other health impairments (OHI), and oppositional defiant disorder (ODD). Visual, hearing, and speech impairments are other categories in which students may qualify for specialized instruction. There are others, but it is most important for an instructional leader to understand the different requirements necessary to qualify for special education under the various categories. It is not enough that only the special education director knows.

504 and Vocational Rehabilitation Act

Many people confuse the rules regarding special education and those regarding 504 plans. There are laws outside of the special education laws that mandate accommodations for some learners. The

American with Disabilities Act (ADA) of 1990 defines accommodations that must be made for some people. (One visible effect of the ADA has been the cutouts that every city must put in sidewalks so that persons have access to streets and sidewalks without having to deal with curbs.) In addition, the Vocational Rehabilitation Act has a Section 504 that prohibits discrimination against individuals with disabilities by school districts and other organizations that receive federal financial assistance.

Section 504 protects persons who: "(1) have a physical or mental impairment that substantially limits one or more of such person's major life activities; (2) have a record of such an impairment; or (3) are regarded as having such an impairment" ([34 CFR 104.3(j)] as quoted in 504 by MNDCFL, p. 3). Major life activities are further defined as functions "such as caring for one's self, performing manual tasks, walking, seeing, hearing, speaking, breathing, learning, and working" ([34 CFR 104.3(j)(2)(ii)] quoted in MNDCFL, p. 3). Sometimes accommodations are made in a classroom that require a written document called a 504 plan, which reflects the law that outlines those modifications.

However, most teachers, parents, and administrators do not realize that a 504 plan is not special education. Special education services are mandated and outlined by IDEIA. There are financial reimbursements, although recognizably inadequate, for some areas of special education. In addition, an IEP must be managed by a licensed special education teacher.

In contrast, 504 modifications are from a different law. Implementing a 504 plan is the responsibility of regular education. There is no financial reimbursement from the federal government to the district for the services provided. A regular education teacher needs to oversee the writing and implementation of the 504 plan that is written to outline the necessary accommodations.

Like an IEP, an effective 504 plan is written with input from professionals and parents. In this case, the individual learning plan (ILP) is designed with a team to outline the modifications necessary in a regular education classroom. Although the federal law does not mandate periodic reviews like it does for special education IEPs, it is important that the ILP be revisited on a periodic basis to monitor the academic progress of the involved student.

The following diagram may help you to understand the relationship between an IDEIA and a 504.

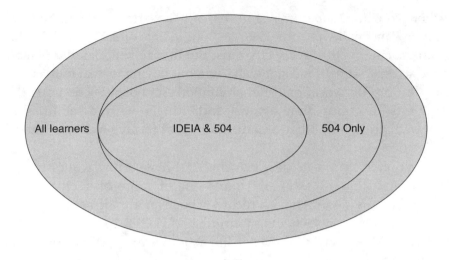

Students may qualify only for modifications under 504 without qualifying for special education. But if students qualify for special education, they would also qualify for interventions under 504. However, the federal mandates of IDEIA take precedence because they are more restrictive.

Although a special education director is often involved with assessing the learning needs of students and directing that a 504 plan be written, the director is not in charge of monitoring the implementation. Implementation is the responsibility of the building administrator because the 504 is a regular education responsibility. It is important for the administrator to be part of the discussions around the identification, to know which students have 504s, and to monitor the accommodations as delivered by the regular education teacher.

Teachers often resent having students in their classrooms with 504 plans because they see it as more work to make accommodations. However, one special education director remarked that if we, as educators, had been more accommodating in meeting the needs of individual students, lawmakers would not have had to enact legislation to make sure it happened.

Legal Knowledge

Case law constantly changes how we have to deliver special education; therefore, it is important that an instructional leader attend legal seminars frequently to stay current with any changes. As cases come before the courts—statewide, circuit level, and the Supreme

Court—interpretations are made about the responsibilities of schools and parents.

One of the areas of concern for administrators is the area of discipline, particularly for those students with behavior disabilities. Administrators must know the state guidelines regarding the number of days a student can be suspended, determine how a disability affects a child's ability to understand the consequences of inappropriate behaviors, and know the intricacies of expulsion proceedings. Because laws are constantly changing, it is important that the administrator knows where to find updated information, perhaps on a department of education Web site, and to have a good working relationship with the special education director.

An effective leader understands how to use resources, both print and people. If in doubt, check it out. Ask other principals, the special education director, or the state department. It is not embarrassing to ask questions. It is embarrassing, however, to make errors that may result in upset parents, teachers, and families or possibly even end in litigation. The administrator must maintain a safe learning environment for all students but must also protect the rights of disabled students, including those with behavioral issues.

Process

Active Participant

One of the key ways a leader can be a director and supporter is to be an active participant in the special education process, from initial referral and assessment to implementation and review of the IEP. That means that a leader must understand all the stages of the process and must not abdicate this responsibility to the special education director and teachers. Because the administrator is the one who is ultimately responsible, it is important to bear that responsibility from an educated, involved position.

It is vital that leaders attend meetings where assessment results are discussed to determine whether a child is eligible for special education. The administrator must be aware of the criteria for and categories of special education and must be willing to enter into the discussion about whether a child qualifies for special education. In particular, if the child does not qualify, the administrator must be able to support the team and help explain to the parents why this is so. It is the role of the administrator, not the teacher, to handle the parents' anger, if there is some. The teachers must feel supported by the administrator.

Dealing With Parents

Another way that a leader is involved in the special education process is in interactions with parents. Parents often see special education as a way for their child to get individual help in certain areas. They often do not realize that there is a label of *disabled* that comes with that identification.

Special education is not an individualized tutoring assistance program with the ultimate goal of getting a child into college. Its purpose is to provide equal access to education for students who have disabilities, not an equal outcome.

The building leader often deals with disgruntled parents. However, it is important to keep in mind that parents of children with special needs are often, whether they are conscious of it or not, grieving the loss of a dream.

When any of us have children, we dream of this child going through life as "normal" and having "normal" experiences. However, when that does not happen, when the child is different, it is a severe loss for the parents. It is the death of their dream. That being the case, parents go through the stages of loss—denial, anger, Bargaining, depression, and acceptance, as defined by Elizabeth Kubler-Ross in her book, *On Death and Dying*.

As parents begin to see that the child is different, the first response is to deny any difference, to make excuses, or to blame others. Next, they get angry, that it "just isn't fair." The anger often gets directed toward the schools. The schools have not done enough or have not done it correctly.

Some parents stay stuck in this stage. Anger feels stronger than sadness because it directs energy toward others. People get angry *at* something or someone. Anger suggests a certain injustice was done *to* them. The opposite would be to experience sadness about the loss, and people would rather be angry than sad because sadness makes them feel more vulnerable.

Bargaining is the third stage. Parents say, "If only . . ." If only the school uses the right modifications, or textbooks, or has a full-time paraprofessional with their child, then the child will be "normal."

The fourth stage is depression. Again this stage makes one feel vulnerable because it is so internal. Being depressed is not an easy place to be. It is the depth of sadness when parents must acknowledge that their child will never match "the dream."

The final stage is acceptance. We have all had dealings with parents whom we admire for their acceptance of how to work with their child. It is my experience that that happens more frequently with children whose difficulties are physical or genetic, rather than emotional or in the learning areas. Parents who have reached acceptance are often active partners, not dictators, in designing the most appropriate program for their child.

As a leader, particularly at initial assessment conferences, it is important to be honest, kind, and forthright. We do not do parents any favors by not telling them the entire truth. Although it is sometimes painful to hear the truth, it is very respectful to parents to be honest. In fact, the sooner parents hear the honesty, the sooner they can get to the acceptance stage about the realities for their child. One special education director believes that one of the reasons districts end up in litigation is because school administrators and/or teachers were not entirely honest with the parents along the way.

Administrators and teachers alike do not like to give out sad news. We would all like to tell each parent with complete accuracy that their child is doing well and earning an A in every class, is a genius, and is well-behaved at all times. However, those children are few and far between and are not usually found in special education.

To convey messages in a respectful fashion, it is sometimes helpful to imagine being the parent on the other side of the table. What is a respectful tone of voice? What body language shows connection and respect? What words are honest yet convey the hard message? Put yourself in their shoes and treat them as you would want to be treated.

In special education and other settings, one way to give difficult news in an honest manner is to describe behavior and patterns of behavior, rather than focusing on abstractions. Also eliminate value judgments about the behavior so the parent does not feel judged. For example, "Sophie will have difficulty processing words with many syllables. She will learn better if she sees them in writing." Parents are more likely to understand that than "Sophie has an auditory processing problem." One can say, "Justin walked over to Martine, used the flat part of his hand, and slapped Martine across the face," rather than "Justin did a bad thing today. He hit Martine."

It is important to describe issues in real English, not special education jargon or in "educationese." Avoid the use of acronyms such as EBD, OCD, and so on. Describe the behavior, not the label.

Reports should be written so that anyone can read them without needing a psychologist or special educator to act as an interpreter. Have a person who is not familiar with the jargon proofread the document before giving it to parents, if there is a question, to make certain that parents will be able to understand it fully.

As a leader it may be necessary to proofread documents before they are distributed to make certain that they are easily understood. It is also important that all documents be written in correct English and that spelling and typing errors have been corrected. We are supposed to be the people training others in correct English and spelling. It looks very unprofessional if documents are given to parents that have errors in them.

Another resource for administrators is Elaine K. McEwan's *How to Deal With Parents Who Are Angry, Troubled, Afraid, or Just Plain Crazy* (1998). One chapter is about defusing such parents. The book also has proactive steps that can be taken to build parental support for the school.

Role With Accountability

In our current climate of accountability, one of the items under close scrutiny is how special education students are tested and counted toward the efforts of the school and district in making adequate yearly progress (AYP) under No Child Left Behind (NCLB). Different states have different criteria. It is very important that leaders understand the criteria within their resident states.

Special education is one of the most vulnerable areas for not making AYP locally and nationally. In addition to understanding the criteria, leaders must then facilitate discussions around data and what to do with them. Which students did not make progress? In which learning areas? Reading? Math? What grade level? What instructional strategies are being used? What best practice strategies should be incorporated? What professional development is needed? What training is needed in looking at data so teachers can monitor this process throughout the year? What training is needed in formative assessments? Interventions? How does one facilitate looking at all the pieces? And, importantly, how does a leader do this without blaming the students and teachers?

Jim Collins (2001) said that great leaders create "a climate where the truth is heard" in a manner that "conducts autopsies, without blame" (p. 88). That means being honest about the issues and directing energies toward resolving them in a manner that allows people to "search for understanding and learning" (p. 78).

Create an Atmosphere of Acceptance

One of the greatest gifts an instructional leader can give to special and regular education is the creation of an environment of acceptance for special education students. It is important to create a climate of acceptance that puts students and their learning as the top priority. It is important that teachers realize that the students' learning is what is important, not their convenience.

It is important for the leader to support special education teachers as well. There is a subtle, or not so subtle, hidden power among teachers that says a person has more status if they teach more students and teach in regular education, particularly in those areas that are tested. Too often special education teachers are not given the same informal esteem as an English teacher, for example, because they do not have as many students.

It is important for a leader to create an atmosphere that recognizes the interlocking importance of all positions. The tasks of special education teachers and social studies teachers are different, for example. Neither is better than the other—just different.

One way to create the IDEIA of a team is to make certain that special education teachers are represented on standing committees in the building, for example. Special education teachers need to be part of activities of the district staff on professional development days and not be doing their own thing.

They need to be represented on all curriculum review teams. Too often curriculum teams exclude exceptional learners as teachers discuss what curriculum should be taught. But it is important for teachers of special needs learners, from the gifted to the autistic, to provide real insight into truly differentiated lesson plans.

Another way to show support is to make certain that regular education teachers are educated as to the meanings of special education. The leader must also make certain that regular education teachers attend IEP meetings. Special education students are still the responsibility of all teachers, not just the case manager, which is sometimes difficult for regular education teachers to accept.

Relationships With Special Educator Directors

Although it is important to have knowledge about special education, it is impossible to know it all. Therefore, a wise leader develops and maintains a healthy relationship with the special education director. The collaboration provides support both for the building administrator and for the director, who often feels like a fireman constantly putting out fires. The director can give good advice, guidance, and support around complicated issues. The special education director is a valuable resource when it comes to specifics about laws, procedures, rules, and the intricacies of special education.

Summary

Special education is a complex system of laws, interpretations, and rights. The purpose is to provide an equal playing field for students with special needs. There are other requirements of schools, in addition, that are proscribed by other statutes. It is vital that a leader be well grounded in knowledge and process. It is important that a leader be intimately involved in the special education process as a participant and as support to students, parents, and staff.

Hanh (1998) reminds us that "In the process of learning, reflecting, and practicing, our view becomes increasingly wise, based on our real experience" (p. 56).

Personal Journal

1. Do I know enough about special education laws and rules? If not, how can I gather more information?

2. How can I work more closely with the special education director and team?

3. What strategies do I have in dealing with parents?

Group Discussion

1. How is the relationship and interaction of regular education and special education? What training needs are apparent?

2. When do regular and special educators get the opportunity to share their expertise and concerns? Do we need training on teaming? Working with paraprofessionals?

9

Understanding Cultural Proficiency

To Thomas L. Friedman, author of *The World Is Flat: A Brief History of the Twenty-First Century* (2005), the "world [is] no longer round—but flat" (p. 11). What he means is that as our world has become increasingly connected, national borders have become more porous, and "because it is flattening and shrinking, Globalization 3.0 is going to be more and more driven not only by individuals but also by a much more diverse—non-Western, non-white—group of individuals. Globalization 3.0 makes it possible for so many more people to plug and play, and you are going to see every color of the human rainbow take part" (p. 11)

In addition, we have parallel, but antithetical movements in which people are gravitating to ethnic descriptions, such as Serb or Ukrainian, as a way of claiming a personal identity in a world that feels increasingly huge and impersonal. In order to have some identity and affiliation, people are rediscovering what it means to be Peruvian, Polish, German, and so on.

In the United States, other than American Indians, or First Nation Peoples, all of us, or our ancestors, have come from other countries and other cultures. We have gathered together in this political structure we call the United States to form a country unlike any other in written history.

Diverse perspectives enrich us all. However, we know that historically that idea has not been embraced, and is still not, by many groups. We enjoy diverse perspectives from different races and different cultures. What we know, in our daily lives as educational leaders, is that embracing diversity and learning about diverse perspectives is a reality. It is important that we gain an understanding of the richness and complexity of the differences as we live in a world where technology has erased some borders.

Some excellent resources for educators are *Cultural Proficiency: A Manual for School Leaders* by Randall B. Lindsey, Kikanza Nuri Robins, and Raymond D. Terrell (2003) and *The Culturally Proficient School: An Implementation Guide for School Leaders* by Randall B. Lindsey, Laraine M. Roberts, and Franklin Campbell Jones (2005). Another important book is *The Middle of Everywhere* by Mary Pipher (2002), which offers some suggestions for incorporating our refugees into American communities. Lisa Delpit's *Other People's Children* (1995) offers suggestions for addressing what she calls the "cultural clash" between teachers and students.

An educational leader must know three things. First, a leader must understand some of the history of immigration and racial classifications, and must understand the forecast for the future because of the ramifications within a school and district. Second, a leader must welcome diverse perspectives as a bonus to us all. Finally, the leader must have a goal as to where the building and district need to go.

Race

Issues about race have been divisive in this country in many arenas—personally, politically, and educationally. However, just as we know that the world is truly not flat, it is important for us to use our scientific knowledge, to take the discussion about race to a new level, to change the old paradigms about that sensitive topic, and to ponder the anthropological argument that "races don't really exist, or more precisely, that the concept of race has no validity as a biological category," according to Carol Mukhopadhyay, a professor in the Department of Anthropology at San Jose State University, and Rosemary C. Henze, an associate professor in the Department of Linguistics and Language Development at San Jose State University (*Kappan,* May 2003, p. 669). Race is not biology; it is a "cultural invention, a culturally and historically specific way of thinking about, categorizing, and treating human beings" (*Kappan,* p. 673).

Anthropologists reject at least three of the fundamental premises of the "old racial ideology: (1) the archaic subspecies concept; (2) the divisibility of contemporary humans into scientifically valid biological groupings; and (3) the link between racial traits and social, cultural, and political status" (*Kappan*, p. 670). Anthropologists have found that populations are ever changing, merging, and shifting. "There have never been any 'pure' races. All human populations are historically specific mixtures of the human gene pool" (*Kappan*, p. 671).

Historically, the definition of race dates to Johann Friedrich Blumenbach in 1795 (80 years before Darwin wrote *Origin of the Species*), who divided all humans into five groups defined by geography and appearance. He fallaciously believed that *Homo sapiens* had been created in a single region and then spread over the globe. Racial diversity arose because people spread to other climates and topographies where the adaptations, such as sickle cell anemia, then became inherited. Black Africans and white Europeans were of equal status based on their common origins. However, he used the white as the model and assumed that all others stemmed from there, creating the system that still compares others by that "ideal." He chose relative physical beauty as his ranking, thinking that the ideal was those from the Caucasian mountains, hence the name "Caucasian" (Gould, 1994, p. 2)

Humans are not divisible into biological races. To be divided, classification must be based on "objective, consistent, and reliable biological criteria . . . which must also have predictive value" (*Kappan*, p. 671). Current classifications "rely on only a few visible, superficial, genetic traits—such as skin color and hair texture—and ignore the remaining preponderance of human variation" (*Kappan*, p. 671). The classification system that is currently used for skin color and hair type, for example, does not always cluster together (*Kappan*, p. 672). Someone could have very dark skin and very curly hair, or someone could have very light skin and very curly hair. There are other traits that are less visible but have far greater significance, such as genetic factors relating to blood types.

"Racial classifications are also unscientific because they are unreliable and unstable over time" (*Kappan*, p. 672). For example, at one time, there were racial classifications of octoroon, mulatto, and black. And now we have Asian/South Pacific Islander. What does that mean? "Estimates suggest that contemporary racial variation accounts for less than 7% of all human genetic variation. U.S. races, then, are not biologically distinct or biologically meaningful, scientifically based groupings of the human species" (*Kappan*, p. 672).

"Race as biology has no scientific value" (*Kappan*, p. 673). The concept of race does not help us to understand other phenomena. "There is no substantial evidence that race, as a biological category . . . [is] causally linked to behavior, to capacities, to individual and group accomplishments, to cultural institutions, or to propensities to engage in any specific activities" (*Kappan*, p. 673). This is particularly important as we look at achievement gaps.

How does this information affect educators and educational leaders? First, it is important to recognize that race is a political, rather than biological, reality. "Race and racism profoundly structure who we are, how we are treated, how we treat others, and our access to resources and rights" (*Kappan*, p. 674). We as educators have the opportunity to change attitudes and the system and erase the divisiveness around racial classifications and conversations. We have the opportunity to look deeper into issues.

Such things as No Child Left Behind (NCLB) force us into using racial labels that help us identify students who are not achieving. But too often we use the labels to blame the victim, by saying "those" children are not as capable. (It was not too long ago that Galton tried to sort mental capabilities by measuring head size—the larger the head, the smarter the individual [http://www.madsci.org/posts/archives/oct2000/970880334.Ns.r.html]). (An interesting book is Stephen Jay Gould's book, *The Mismeasure of Man* (1981), which talks about how IQ tests were developed and practiced on the immigrants in the early 1920s in a fashion that perpetuated racial stereotypes.) Is using race as a category similar to equating head size with intelligence? If those categories disappeared, how would we reshape our thinking?

"It is also important to discuss how macroracial categories also serve society. By looking at the descriptors of our society's interaction with the concept of race, we can witness how we, as a culture, have thought about race" (*Kappan*, p. 675). The label is not inherently bad or good; it is what people do with the label that is important. It can help us to look for trends or possible affects of education to eradicate racism (*Kappan*, p. 676).

As educators it is important for us to "shift the conversation from biology to culture" (*Kappan*, p. 676). We can "dismantle the myth of race as biology . . . to shift our focus to analyzing the social, economic, political, and historical conditions" that perpetuate social inequality. Also, by recognizing the impermanence of race, one must understand that "culture, acting collectively, and humans, acting individually, can make races disappear" (*Kappan*, p. 676).

Following is a discussion about "descriptors of society's interaction with race" in this country. By examining our verbal descriptors, we can get a sense of where we have been. Prior to the 1950s, we lived in a time of *segregation*. The races were to be distinct and separate. During the 1950s we moved toward *desegregation*, particularly with the landmark decision of *Brown v. Board of Education*. We created certain situations to put races together in an equal setting, schools being one of them. The 1960s were a time of *integration;* the 1970s were described by *multiculturalism.* In the 1980s we talked about *diversity* and tried to learn about individual cultures in an additive approach, where we learned about cultures individually (Lindsey et al., 2003, pp. 9–11). However, as Mary Pipher, the author of *Middle of Everywhere* (2002), said, "even idealizing other cultures can be a form of racism" (p. 330).

From the 1990s and beyond we have come through *cultural competence* to *cultural proficiency* now (Lindsey et al., 2003, pp. 9–11). As we think of the discussion of the anthropological fallacy of race, of changing our discussion from race to culture, it is important that we achieve *cultural proficiency*, which "is an approach to addressing diversity issues that goes beyond political correctness . . . [to] reveal greater depth of knowledge, introspection, and sincere intent than may be found in politically correct responses" (p. 13). Cultural proficiency involves "expanding the paradigm for culture to encompass everything that people believe and everything that they do that identifies them as members of a group and distinguishes that group from other groups" (p. 27). "It is not an off-the-shelf program. . . . It is an approach for responding to the environment shaped by its diversity" (p. 5).

Achieving cultural proficiency is both an internal and external journey. People must learn about diverse perspectives, which is where the multicultural approach stopped. In addition, educators must act to "provide mutual support to one another so that every educator feels understood and respected for who he or she is and to the groups to which they belong" (p. 15).

In *Cultural Proficiency: A Manual for School Leaders*, Randall B. Lindsey, Kikanza Nuri Robins, and Raymond D. Terrell (2003) describe the need for what they call "an inside out approach that focuses first on those who are insiders to the school, encouraging them to reflect on their own individual understandings and values" (p. 39). They describe a continuum to assist in looking at differences:

1	2	3	4	5

1. Cultural Destructiveness—"See the Difference, Stomp It Out" — Eliminates another's culture.

2. Cultural Incapacity—"See the Difference, Make It Wrong" — One's own culture is superior.

3. Cultural Blindness—"See the Difference, Act Like You Don't" — "This is the belief that culture and color make no difference and that all people are the same." (p. 98)

4. Cultural Precompetence—"See the Difference, Respond to It Inappropriately"—"People and organizations . . . recognize that their skills and practices are limited when interacting with other cultural groups" (p. 99). They recognize differences but may not provide support to those who are "others."

5. Cultural Competence—"See the Difference, Understand the Difference That Difference Makes"— "This includes acceptance and respect for difference; continuing self-assessment regarding culture; careful attention to the dynamics of difference; continuous expansion of cultural knowledge and resources; and a variety of adaptations to belief systems, policies, and practices." (p. 99)

It is helpful for educational leaders to look at themselves and their staff to see where they lie along this continuum. It is important work to take people where they are on the continuum and move them forward. This is work that will never be done.

Immigration

Apart from race, another source of rich cultural diversity has been from immigrants to this country. Historically, if interested, an educational leader can research the history of our immigration and immigration laws. In relatively recent history, in 1924 and 1928, the United States passed laws establishing quota systems that still influence our immigration patterns today. The quotas favored people who were light skinned, light haired, and predominantly Christian.

The U.S. population "has always been multiracial, and it is becoming even more diverse now" than at the time of our founding (http://www.prb.org/). In 1900 about 90% of the population was white, and nearly all of the remaining 10% was African American. At the end of the 20th century, non-Hispanic whites represented 72% of the population and the minority population was more "diverse as well as more numerous." Non-Hispanic African Americans and

Hispanics account for about 12% of the population, and Asian and Pacific Islanders account for nearly 4% (http://www.prb.org/).

Currently the United States is seeing a more dramatic shift than before in its population with new immigrants from different areas of the world and in the growing numbers of populations that are nonwhite. Between 1980 and 1998, nearly three-quarters "of all new immigrants came from Asia and Latin America, while about 20 percent came from Europe and about 4 percent from Africa" (Saenz, 2004, p. 16).

Immigrant groups will continue to grow, particularly from Africa and Asia. The Census Bureau projects that the minority population will grow from 28% in 1999 to 45% in 2050. By 2010, Hispanics will outnumber non-Hispanic African Americans to become the nation's largest minority population. "Hispanics will make up nearly 15 percent of the U.S. population in 2010 and nearly 25 percent by 2050. By 2060, non-Hispanic whites are projected to be less than one-half of all Americans. By 2100, nonwhites and Hispanics are projected to make up 60 percent of the U.S. population, with Hispanics alone accounting for 33 percent" (Saenz, 2004, p. 17).

The number of Latinos in the United States more than doubled between 1980 and 2000, accounting for 40% of the growth in the country's population during that period. In 2003, the U.S. Census Bureau designated Latinos as the nation's largest minority group, an amazing event considering that in 1980 the Latino population was only slightly more than one-half the size of the African American population (Saenz, 2004, p. x).

The United States has seen itself as a "melting pot." The philosophy of "give me your tired, your poor, your hungry" is being tested as we welcome more people who look less like the people who arrived on the *Mayflower*. Our populations are changing to incorporate not only different skin colors, but also different religious beliefs, which, after September 11, 2001, causes bias as these beliefs are identified with certain populations who are perceived as a threat to what it means to be an "American."

Another difference for schools is that some of our students are coming to us without having been educated in their native countries. Some have been forced to live in refugee camps, and others are from nomadic cultures where education is about daily survival, not about reading and writing. It is one thing to teach literacy skills to someone who is literate in one culture and quite another to teach literacy to someone who is preliterate in their native language.

Another difference is that students may be able to speak several languages because of their past. English may be the third or fourth spoken language, but writing has not been learned in any language. It is important to remember that "in spite of their disadvantages, refugees have lower drop-out rates and better grades than native-born kids" (Pipher, 2002, p. 115).

Pipher (2002) described mistakes we make out of JPI—Just Plain Ignorance—particularly as we deal with immigrant families. She listed 10 common beliefs of JPI:

1. Refugees are ignorant and have no formal education. *Many have college educations in their own lands, but our laws keep them out of those professions.*

2. The United States takes in most of the world's refugees, when in fact we take in *less than 1%.*

3. Most refugees are here illegally. *Not so.*

4. Newcomers are taking American jobs. *Truth be told, the immigrants are filling jobs that Americans will not take—fast-food, cab drivers, parking lot attendants, for example.*

5. Newcomers do not pay taxes. *Not true. In fact some who work more than one job at minimum wage pay a higher percentage of wages to taxes than many in the middle class and certainly more than the upper class.*

6. Tax dollars go to teach refugees in their own language. *There is little money for ELL (English Language Learner) support in schools, and it is cut off after a very short time.*

7. Newcomers do not want to learn English. *Most refugees try to learn quickly, and this may be their third or fourth language.*

8. Most refugees end up on welfare. *In fact, most are working within a month of their arrival, and do what Pipher calls "3-D" work—difficult, dirty, and dangerous.*

9. Anyone who wants to can come to America. *In fact, there are strict rules and quotas.*

10. Why don't they go back to where they belong? *Refugees do not have that option. They left in fear of their lives and the lives of their families* (Pipher, 2002, pp. 334–336).

Pipher gives some pointers for working with people for whom English is a new language:

1. Use short, simple sentences and speak slowly.

2. Pause frequently. Write it down. Immigrants often have a sponsor who can help them read. In addition, a hard copy gives the immigrant something to refer to, if necessary.

3. Do not use jargon or professional language.

4. Give a little information at a time. Do not overload people.

5. Good manners are important to demonstrate regard and respect.

6. Take time to work with people.

7. Try to learn to say "hello" in their language. Try to learn something about their culture, for example, if there is a difference in greetings. In some cultures, for example, women do not shake hands, particularly with men who are not their husbands.

8. Pay attention to nonverbals. Do not look at your watch. Give people your attention.

9. Use interpreters wisely. In some cultures it is insulting to use children as interpreters because it inverts the relationship of parent/child. In that situation, hire an interpreter so the parent is not shamed. (Pipher, 2002, pp. 353–355)

However, as Pipher said, "Schools are often where kids experience their first racism and learn about the socioeconomic split in our country. There is the America of children with violin lessons, hockey tickets, skiing trips, and zoo passes, and there is the America of children in small apartments whose parents work double shifts" (p. 114).

All of the issues surrounding the artificial construct of race, culture, increasing diverse populations, and what it means to be human are complicated. Pipher said, "Our economy and our technology have changed much more rapidly than our conceptions about what it means to be human. In our rapidly changing world, we need research about the effects of global meld on people" (p. 305).

Education is important. "School may be overwhelming at first, but it is school that will enable children to make it in America" (Pipher, 2002, p. 115).

Other Issues

There are other issues around cultural proficiency, but this book cannot address them all. We have differences along religious lines, sexual orientation, physical ability, socioeconomic status, and so on. However, an aura of cultural proficiency permeates the recognition that diverse perspectives are important and need to be recognized and embraced.

Accountability

In our current climate of accountability an educational leader needs to be aware of data pressures in two particular areas: our English language learner (ELL) population and in examining racial categories, as defined by the federal government. Although the task is complex and we would all prefer that all students, regardless of race, socioeconomic status (SES), or culture, achieve equally, there is an achievement gap that all administrators must address. It is important to use the categories in a manner that does not perpetuate racial and cultural stereotypes but instead helps us to eradicate prejudice and bias to educate all students equally.

However, an administrator must learn how to look at data, how to ask the right questions, and how to program for students within a particular setting and building. One must be wise when looking at studies and statistics, because, as pointed out by Gerald Bracey (2000) in *Bail Me Out*, "It used to be that the only data of concern to teachers and administrators were those concerning budgets and personnel. No more. School people who do not know what the data actually say about schools are vulnerable not only to half-truths and spun data, but to the perseveration of myths about schools. Some of these myths are remarkably long lived in spite of data refuting them" (p. 4).

We are held accountable for all students to learn in an accountability model that favors high socioeconomic, white populations.

In addition, an administrator must examine data for No Child Left Behind that are disaggregated along five racial categories, which is interesting because, in designing that law, our educated politicians fell into the same seductive trap of the artificial construct of trying to define race.

In fact, what we know today is that "Individuals cannot reliably be 'raced,' partly because the criteria are so subjective and unscientific" (*Kappan*, p. 672). Educators should be careful, "However, to avoid 'biologizing' the classification; that is we must avoid assuming genetic explanations for racial differences in behaviors and educational outcomes or even diseases" (*Kappan*, p. 676).

Unequal housing, employment, and education continue to be plagued by the artificial constructs of race. Richard Rothstein, a research associate with the Economic Policy Institute in Washington, DC, said in a recent article in the *Kappan* that "the influence of social-class characteristics is probably so powerful that schools cannot overcome it, no matter how well trained their teachers and no matter how well designed their instructional programs and climates" (*Kappan*, 2004, p. 107).

"Because of the high stakes attached to standardized tests in recent years, schools and teachers are under enormous pressure to raise students' test scores. The more pressure there has been, the less reliable these scores have become. In part, the tests themselves don't really measure the gap in the achievement of high standards because high standards (such as the production of good writing and the development of research skills and analysis) are expensive to test, and public officials are reluctant to spend the money" (*Kappan*, 2004, p. 108).

We know that students of color continue to perform more poorly than do white students. There are two issues here: First, our education system teaches and assesses in a system that is linked to middle-class, white culture. Books describe the white experience, even the white male experience. Our tests, such as intelligence tests, contain subtle biases. Our standardized tests contain questions that are culturally laden in such a subtle fashion.

Second, our society is permeated by racism in a manner that keeps people from equal opportunities in employment and housing. We know that although our society is becoming more diverse, the power and money continue to be held by the white culture.

Schools have been thought to be the great equalizers for the ills of society. Justice Thurgood Marshall and friends worked hard to integrate schools with *Brown v. Board of Education* with the hopes that access to a decent education would open the doors for access to equality in employment and housing. That has not materialized, as we have seen by the recent follow-up studies of 50 years after *Brown*.

Rothstein suggests three tracks to make significant progress: (1) Raise the quality of instruction in elementary and secondary schools; (2) "expand the definition of schooling to include crucial out-of-school hours in which families and communities now are the sole influences"; and (3) implement social and economic policies that will enable children to attend school more equally ready to learn" (*Kappan*, 2004, p. 109). He concluded with "For nearly half a century, the association of social and economic disadvantage with a student achievement gap has been well known to economists, sociologists, and educators. However, most have avoided the obvious implications of this understanding; raising the achievement of lower-class children requires the amelioration of the social and economic conditions of their lives, not just school reform. Perhaps we are now ready to reconsider this needlessly neglected opportunity" (*Kappan*, 2004, p. 110).

However, schools are not the only entities that need to be held accountable when it comes to serving our children. Robert Evans (2005) recently wrote an article for the *Kappan* entitled "Reframing the Achievement Gap," in which he discussed the idea that schools are scapegoated in the discussion about the achievement gap. He believed that there needs to be a larger discussion and an "honest acknowledgement of the complexities of the achievement gap and the realities of schooling" (p. 587). We as a culture "would begin not by asking how schools should address the achievement gap but by asking what conditions need to be in place so that schools can do so. First, it would look *beyond schools* in seeking ways to prevent the gap. Next it would consider what must be done *for schools* so that they can do their part once children arrive. Then it would turn to what must be done *by schools* themselves. At every step, it would balance wishes against realities" (p. 587).

How Does an Effective School Leader Create a Climate of Cultural Proficiency?

"Culturally proficient leaders are guided by theory in developing first a vision and then a mission that serves the needs of all students" (Lindsey et al., 2003, p. 53). Too often our past efforts at learning about diversity have been to acquire knowledge and awareness for adults. However, that did not translate into academic achievement for students. With the current mandates to achieve academic progress for all, and with our current technology tools with drill-down software, we are able to diagnose and target specific areas of need and then target professional development to fit those needs.

A culturally proficient leader, therefore, provides a framework for adults to take that inner and outer journey, to look at where they are on the continuum of cultural proficiency in the context of a school that is embedded in culture, and then provide an outward framework to discover "how and why we learn about others, engage in team learning, and examine data for the purpose of making informed changes in school practices" (p. 55).

Leaders must do several things: First, they must provide the vision that cultural proficiency is a goal. The leader helps to establish the vision in conjunction with the staff and community. Sometimes the staff and community wax nostalgic in wanting "the good old days." There was no such thing. That was an illusion created by those in power, those with advantages. It is more important that we work toward talking about, recognizing, and cherishing the fact that we are not all the same.

Second, leaders must use data to provide awareness to staff. Leaders use academic data, demographic data, and community data about our world. It is important to understand how students are learning.

Third, leaders provide opportunities for targeted professional development based on need. If there is a need to understand issues of diversity, then the leader helps do that. If there is a need to understand divergent teaching strategies, such as those of the National Urban Alliance, the leader should research them.

Fourth, leaders provide opportunities for community involvement—the whole community. It is important to both educate and support the entire educational community. That may mean educating white parents about changing demographics as well as meeting with immigrant parents with an interpreter in their home to explain how American schools operate.

Summary

It is important to work toward cultural proficiency. It is a change in thinking to broaden the discussion of *culture* to include more than just race and country of origin—to include disabilities, sexual orientation, and socioeconomics.

The journey toward cultural proficiency is one that is both internal—examining one's own attitudes and beliefs—and external—looking at how we can all benefit and learn from one another. The paradoxical goal of embracing diverse perspectives while working toward common goals of student achievement for all is complex at best. As educators we need to continue to learn, to look at data with an educated eye, and to keep talking.

In her book *The Measure of Our Success: A Letter to My Children and Yours*, Marian Wright Edelman (1992) states that "race and gender are shadows; and that character, self-discipline, determination, attitude, and service are the substance of life" (p. 7).

Personal Journal

1. Where would I put myself on the continuum of cultural proficiency?

2. What gift have I received from people from other cultures?

3. What is one thing I can do to embrace diverse perspectives in my school?

Group Discussion

1. What work needs to be done in our school and district to change the culture from "blaming the victim" to using data to target instruction and professional development?

2. What are strengths we can build upon in our school and district?

10

Making the Most of Meetings

We have all been in meetings that were well run and accomplished a task. We have also been in meetings that were pointless and a complete waste of time. Meetings are an important part of an administrator's life, yet managing an effective meeting is a mixture of skill and art that is not addressed or taught in most administrative training programs.

School administrators might be surprised if they ever calculated the amount of time spent in meetings each week. We sit through meetings of different types with different groups and without thinking about the actual process of constructing an appropriate meeting.

We often just set a time for a meeting and then gather people together and proceed. We have not been trained to think about setting an agenda based on the purpose or length of the meeting, the participants involved, or the desired outcome. All of those considerations are important in running an effective meeting. In this chapter we will discuss some management strategies for effective meeting design and facilitation for the educational leader.

Considerations in Planning the Agenda

Purpose of Meetings

One consideration in planning is the **purpose** of meeting:

1. Is it to **impart** information? Examples of informational meetings are staff meetings, professional development

sessions, and presentations to the community group about accountability data.

2. Is it to **gather** information? Examples of information-gathering meetings are groups structured as task forces to gather data on data management systems or groups to review several programs to discover attributes of the best one.

3. Is it to **reach a decision**? Student assistance teams, committees that set next year's school calendar, and curriculum review committees are examples of this type of meeting.

4. Is it to **build an understanding or collaboration**? This would include meetings with community groups, site team meetings, and PTA meetings, which work toward collaboration.

5. Is it to **mediate conflict**? Resolving conflicts between teachers and students, mediating differences between two staff members, or intervening between two students who are getting ready to fight are examples of conflict mediation.

Participants

Another consideration is to think about the **power base or knowledge of the participants**. Meetings may be with:

1. **Peers.** Peers are people who have the same degree of power and knowledge. An example would be a meeting of fifth-grade teachers to discuss academic progress. If the only people at the table are fifth-grade teachers, theoretically they are equal in power and in knowledge. There is some hidden and personal power that comes in to play, but, by organizational structure, they are considered peers.

2. Those with **less expertise or power.** An example of a difference in power is staff meetings that are led by the building principal. Teachers and principals do not have the same level of power. When planning the meeting, the principal must take that into account. Another consideration is if the purpose of the meeting is to share information with people of unequal expertise. If so, the facilitator will have to build in time for sharing background knowledge.

3. Those with **more expertise or power**. Sometimes we lead meetings with those who are our superiors in the organizational chart. Examples are task forces; standing school board committees; and or fact-finding committees with legislators, mayors, teachers, and administrators. As with those with less expertise, it is important to develop some sort of common awareness around the topic.

4. Those **outside the organization**. Sometimes administrators chair meetings with community members who are outside the organization. The power base may be immaterial, but it is then important to establish a common base of knowledge.

Time Considerations

Another consideration is the **length of time** that will be devoted to the meeting.

Meetings are structured differently depending on the length of time they are scheduled to take. How long do you want the meeting to last?

1. 1 to 1 ½ hours?

2. A half-day?

3. One day or more?

4. Or is it a standing committee that meets on a regular basis?

In the following discussion you will find sample agendas and hints to consider when thinking about the elements of a meeting.

Setting Agendas

Depending on the length of the meeting, the purpose of the meeting, and the participants involved, setting the agenda is different.

In general, plan time for introductions, for establishing the purpose of the meeting, and for closure/recap activities. Introductions are important even if the participants work in the same district, particularly if there is a possibility that people have not met or do not know what position people hold. It is important to know who is in the room, why they are there, and what they want from the meeting.

Think of the meeting as a spiral. At the beginning, goals are established. Then the meeting does its work and begins a circular journey. The end of the meeting recaps the purpose of the meeting and what was accomplished, and hopefully everyone comes away with a new level of understanding.

When setting agendas it is important to think about the desired outcome. Stephen Covey (1994), author of *First Things First,* talks about "beginning with the end in mind" (pp. 98–144). Are people to reach a decision? Or is the meeting to facilitate communication? Or is it to share information?

The purpose of the meeting may determine whether there is one item or many on the agenda. For some meetings, the agendas often set themselves because the meeting revolves around a certain topic. For example, a task force might get together to discuss what to do about the fact that many students come late to their first-period class. In that case, the facilitator would start with a general statement as to the purpose of the meeting and what the desired outcome will be. The facilitator then opens the meeting with discussion questions and closes the meeting by summarizing what was accomplished.

If the purpose of the meeting is to share information, the agenda is set by listing the items that must be discussed and allotting a certain amount of time per item. Again the facilitator would begin by presenting an overview and close by summarizing what was covered.

If the purpose of the meeting is to build collaboration, the facilitator would begin with an overview comment. Then the facilitator would ask the participants to brainstorm the issues around the topic. The facilitator would begin to see patterns and want to try to cluster ideas around larger topics. The next step would be to discuss the competing values. At the end of the meeting, or series of meetings, a decision should be made. It should be made clear who is to make the final decision. Is it the role of the group? of the administration? of the school board?

For standing committees, the agenda may be suggested by several members of the committee. The facilitator would try to assign a respectful amount of time to each topic and guide the discussion. The facilitator would monitor the time and provide opening and closure for the meeting. One tool that is particularly helpful for standing committees is to develop a "shared folder" on the computer with access for the members of the committee. Then each committee member could enter agenda items without having to go through another party, such as a secretary. A shared folder negates the need for one person to put items on the agenda. This is helpful so that some items are not lost or forgotten.

How much time is to be allotted to each agenda item is to be decided by the facilitator, because not all items should be treated equally. Too often we start at the top of a list and work down without prioritizing. Instead, take care of important items first so that adequate time can be devoted to the discussion. Leave the "memo" items until the end of the agenda so that if someone has to leave before the meeting is over, they will not miss the important discussion. (A "memo" item is something that could be addressed in memo form and does not necessarily need discussion. Examples are times of conferences and when field trips are scheduled. In fact, it can be used as a management tool to create an agenda so that certain parties are there—or not.)

Sample Agendas: General Considerations

Following are some sample timelines. The amount of time devoted to opening and closing activities will vary depending on the size of the group. If the group is large (more than 15 people), be sure to add more time for introductions and to the recap, so that everyone has a voice at the beginning and the end. Getting people to speak at the beginning makes it more likely that people will be speaking throughout the meeting.

Likewise, it is also important to put closure to the meeting by quickly going around the room for any final comments from all participants. If there are hidden agendas or unresolved issues, this provides another opportunity to air those opinions. Giving each person an opportunity to speak at the end helps to cement their commitment to the outcome of the group.

For a Short Meeting of 1 to 1 ½ Hours

It is helpful to have written agendas for groups. If possible, the agenda should be dispersed electronically before the meeting starts. If not, it can be available as people arrive, or it can be posted on a SmartBoard, white board, or flip chart. If tools such as SmartBoards are available, it is efficient to take notes as the meeting proceeds; then the minutes are already completed and need only be edited for sentence structure and grammar. It is helpful at any meeting to have a recorder who is someone other than the facilitator. It is difficult to run a meeting, particularly if there are more than five or six people, and take notes at the same time.

Samples

Short Meeting (1 to 1/2 hours)

1.	Introductions:	5–10 minutes
2.	Purpose and goal of meeting:	5 minutes
3.	Agenda items:	45–50 minutes
4.	Recap of accomplishments:	5 minutes
5.	Go around the room and ask each person for any final comments	
6.	Establish next meeting date, if necessary:	2 minutes

Half-Day or Daylong Meetings

1.	Introductions:	5–10 minutes
2.	Purpose of the meeting:	5 minutes
3.	Agenda item:	60 minutes
4.	Break:	15 minutes
5.	Agenda:	60 minutes
6.	Lunch:	30–75 minutes

If lunch is brought in, a half-hour is enough time.
If people go out, it takes about 1 to 1 1/2 hours

7.	Agenda:	60 minutes
8.	Break:	15
9.	Agenda:	60
10.	Closure	

If the meeting is only a half-day, closure activities would occur after item 5—a recap and closure.

Standing Meetings

Usually groups that have standing meetings will schedule about an hour for the meeting. Standing committees may be an advisory group, such as a principal's advisory, a site council, or curriculum review committees.

1. Introductions. Make certain that any new members are introduced and welcomed.

2. Hand out minutes from the last meeting or provide a recap of what has happened to date.

3. Purpose of that day's meeting.

4. Work.

5 Closure: Establish work responsibilities and set the next meeting dates.

Facilitation

Effective meetings do not run themselves. An effective meeting is *facilitated* by someone who is in charge and is conscious of all of the previously mentioned considerations. In addition, the person should understand and use facilitation skills, taking into consideration the people in the room, the timing, and the purpose of the meeting. The person should also have knowledge about meeting behavior and group process.

Group process is the topic of many books. One excellent resource is *The Adaptive School: A Sourcebook for Developing Collaborative Groups* (1999) by Robert J. Garmston and Bruce M. Wellman.

Following are some considerations for good facilitators.

1. Skilled meeting leaders understand the **dynamics of group process**. They understand formal and informal power, how to get all participants to talk, and how to quiet the one who tries to monopolize the conversation.

A skilled facilitator will understand that the synergy of combining individuals into a group may be different than the actions or viewpoints of each individual participant.

A good facilitator, by definition, must be a good listener. To put all the pieces together, a facilitator must be able to listen to the conversation, understand the spoken and unspoken messages, and try to frame the ideas in terms of the discussion at hand.

2. Facilitators know that different **groups act differently** because they have different needs. Following are some examples:

   a. "Take care of me"—Each member contributes independently to the outcome. An example is when representatives from various buildings come together to set the school calendar for the following year. Each person has independent ideas.

b. "Take care of us"—In this case the interdependence and interactions of the group motivate people to work together. A staff meeting is an example.

c. "Take care of our values"—The values drive the goals, clarity, and accomplishments for the task at hand. An example is a curriculum review committee that is formed when a group of language arts teachers come together to establish the articulated curriculum (Garmston & Wellman, 1999, p. 31).

3. A skilled facilitator has some **basic tools to elicit responses and move the process forward.** Garmston and Wellman (1999) believe that groups run better when each member has these skills, but it may be up to the facilitator to teach them to the group. Therefore, it is necessary for the leader to have the following skills:

a. Pausing—Allow "wait time" for processing. This helps students and adults alike.

b. Paraphrasing—This is valuable because it allows reflection and establishes clarity, establishes that all in the group have the same understanding. It allows for probing deeper into ideas.

c. Probing for specificity—Ask deeper questions if responses seem vague. Ask for clarification of terms; vague nouns and pronouns; and vague action words, rule words, comparisons, and universal quantifiers. Sometimes we assume that every one knows the meaning of an acronym or standard practice, when that is not true.

d. Pay attention to self and others—Be aware of what is said, how it is said, and how others are receiving the message, both for yourself and members of the group.

e. Presume positive intentions—Assume that the intentions of others are well meaning and honorable, because this establishes a positive tone for the meeting and will go far to create a successful meeting.

f. Pursue a balance between advocacy and inquiry—It is important to be able to advocate for an idea and yet ask for the opinion of others to stretch one's thinking (Garmston & Wellman, 1999, pp. 37–47).

4. Most of all, facilitators are **self-aware** and can guide a process without dominating it (Garmston & Wellman, 1999, p. 92). It is important to know the purpose of the meeting, the participants, and the facilitator's role. It is important for the facilitator to understand personal values so those values are not the only ones in the room.

5. Leaders must **define the charge** of the group. Is it the task of the group to provide input? Gather data? Make recommendations? Develop a creative solution? It is important to be clear about the desired end product so committee members are there for the right reason and can be comfortable with the outcome.

6. As part of the charge of the group, leaders must **describe who gets to make the decision**. Is it the charge of the group to gather ideas, provide input, or solve problems? Or is the task of the group to come to a resolution and make a decision? If the group is to make a decision, who decides? The chair of the meeting? Is it by consensus? Is it the majority? Is this a decision that has to go to another group for input or approval? Does this need school board approval? Principal approval?

For example, if a committee is given the charge to look at ways the district can save money, it is important to set the ground rules at the outset of meeting. The group is to work toward understanding what it is that the district does, what it values, and the costs of various programs; in general, the task is to gather data. Then it is their charge to make recommendations to the superintendent, who will work with his administrative team to prepare recommendations for the school board. It is important for the committee to know at the outset of the process that the school board makes the final decision, not the committee. It is also important for the committee to understand all the steps that must happen before a final decision is made.

Another example is setting the parameters for a committee that is part of a hiring process. An administrator chairs the interview committee for hiring a new teacher. It is important to let the group know that their purpose is to provide input and the final decision will be made by whoever is charged with that responsibility, be it the superintendent, the human resources director, or the principal.

7. **Design the susrroundings.** Participants tend to give more favorable feedback to gatherings where the physical surroundings are amenable and comfortable. How many times have you been uncomfortable in a meeting because it was too

crowded? Too hot? Too cold? The seats too hard? Not enough food?

Prior to the meeting, it is wise for the person in charge to visit the meeting site to make certain that the tables are set up in an appealing fashion; the temperature is regulated; refreshments, such as coffee and water, are available; the technology is working; and paper and pens are available. It is also wise for the leader who is going to an unfamiliar space to bring equipment such as laptop, whiteboard pens, and a flip chart. Too many times I have checked out a meeting site a few days ahead only to find that another meeting had been held there in the interim and the supplies had all been moved.

It is important to create a positive seating arrangement. Seating should be arranged so that everyone has good eye contact. Everyone should be able to look straight ahead, causing less back and neck soreness. Having good sight lines fosters engagement in the proceedings. Try to set up the tables so that pillars and other obstructions are minimized. People who cannot see or hear without a struggle tend to disengage and devalue the outcome of the meeting.

Avoid rooms with fans or fluorescent noise. If there is a hum from fans, lights, or other appliances in the room, participants have to expend energy unconsciously to block out the background noise so that they can hear what is occurring in the meeting. If the noise is loud enough that people mention it, then they are consciously trying to block the sound. Either turn the fans off or find a different room.

8. **Develop meeting norms**. Meeting norms are helpful if the group is a standing committee or if it is going to deal with some contentious topics.

Keep the norms simple and few in number. People will forget them if there are more than four or five. If the group meets more than once, the norms can be posted in the room or printed on the top of each agenda as a constant reminder.

One way to establish the norms of the group is to present a sample list of standard norms at the first meeting and ask the participants to respond. By providing a sample, people do not have to take the time to create one from scratch and can spend their time more productively on the task at hand.

Following are some common norm examples to choose from:

- Respect each other
- Only one person speaks at a time

- Value other people's opinions
- Every one will have an opportunity to share
- Conflict will be dealt with in a professional manner
- Conversations related to the meeting will stay in the room
- Meetings will end on time
- Always bring chocolate!

Once a list has been compiled and the discussion around the topic seems to have waned, meaning that the ideas are all expressed, the leader needs to get consensus that these are the norms of the group. "Does everyone agree that they can adhere to these norms?" If there is silence, one can infer agreement, but because this is important, go around to each person and ask if they can agree. If someone cannot agree, then rework the norms. (Hint: If they have difficulty establishing norms, they will have difficulty resolving other more potent conflicts.)

Other Facilitation Strategies. Following are some strategies that are helpful to learn, and overlearn, so that they can be used seamlessly as needed.

1. *The parking lot:* Educators, and possibly other professionals as well, have a tendency to rush to solution before they ever define the problem adequately. Consequently, they solve the wrong problem and become frustrated with group processes because they say, "We've done this before and nothing changes." Therefore, it is very important to understand the real problem.

A grade-level team is looking at the math scores for that grade. The scores are not what teachers had hoped they would be. The participants immediately start suggesting purchasing a new curriculum, adding supplemental materials, using a new computer program, or blaming parents for not helping with homework. The list goes on. However, the group did not take time to analyze the information in depth to discover that, because the math series is heavily language-based, the issue is that the reading skills of the students are not adequate. Purchasing new math materials may make some difference but will not address the real issue.

So when people start rushing to solution, build a "parking lot," which can be as simple as a sheet of flip-chart paper or a space on the white board, to write down ideas that are ahead of their time, or a little off-task, or something that needs more discussion. Let people know that "These are good ideas. We need to preserve them. However, we need to make certain we are defining the problem adequately so that we derive the appropriate solutions to the real problem. When we feel the problem is truly defined, we'll come back to these items to see if they will help us." Be sure to include a "parking lot'" page in the minutes so people feel validated. People will respect the fact that their opinions were regarded, and yet the meeting did not get off-task.

2. *Intervening:* It is common for meetings to go off-task. It is the task of the leader to keep the focus of the meeting in mind. It is also the task of the leader to decide if the off-task ideas are actually helpful. If they are, use a "parking lot" to keep them for further discussion. If not, the leader can refocus back to what was stated as the charge at the opening of the meeting.

An example is a meeting to learn the differentiation strategy of "scaffolding." Someone brought up how they use exit cards, which triggered a comment from another person. Using exit cards is not part of scaffolding and is not necessarily an idea for a parking lot. Respectfully, one can say, "These are very good ideas. However, it is my task to keep us focused on the topic of today. May we go back to. . .?"

However, some of the "birdwalks" are the types of ideas that bring fresh air into a stale argument. It will be the task of the facilitator to decide if that is true. The ideas could be the topic of study for a task force, which could then be brought back later to the larger group.

For example, a group is studying the implementation of a new student management system. A person in the group brings up the name of a resource that no one else has heard of. The facilitator may ask for more information, or ask for a task force to study it and bring it back to the larger group.

The facilitator has to decide **when** to intervene. Some hints as to when to intervene are as follows:

- If the same basic idea has been stated three times and it seems as though everyone wants to give their own example
- If ideas are personal, rather than topical
- If ideas become targeted toward an individual
- If it feels like people are airing "dirty laundry" or blaming parents or the administration—the usual targets
- If people start fidgeting in their chairs, giving the hint they are disengaged.

The leader must decide **how** to intervene. One strategy is to make a general statement. Some sample general statements are, "Thanks for sharing ideas. However, the focus for today is . . ."; "My role as facilitator is to keep us on task. Can we go back to the topic at hand?"; "There are three topics on the floor right now. Would it be okay if we put these two on the parking lot because the focus of today is. . . ."

Another strategy is to describe behavior: "I see that some of you have not spoken yet. Bill, what is your stance?"; "I sense that the group is (frustrated, happy, uncomfortable) with where we are. It would be helpful if we clarify that before we go on." Then generate a list of things that are causing the distraction. It may be necessary to deal with the distractions before the meeting can progress.

3. *How to focus attention, particularly for meetings of a day or more.* A good meeting starts with the leader calling it to order and focusing attention on the task at hand. For long meetings, it is important to establish routines and procedures that signal the call to attention. For example, use a pleasant-sounding bell; switch the lights off and on; or raise a hand and, as people come to attention, have everyone get quiet and raise their hands. Be careful not to use a signal that is disrespectful to the age level of the group. For example, a loud whistle is jarring and more appropriate to a football field, and clapping hands could be seen as very elementary and condescending to some groups.

Some leaders use physical locations, such as standing in one specific place whenever attention should be focused toward the leader. For example, at the beginning of the day, after breaks, after lunch, and so on, the leader would go to a certain spot and begin. Gradually people would come to understand that, when this happens, it is time to stop private conversations and get back to the meeting.

4. *Brainstorming and visual strategies.* Visual strategies are useful tools to stimulate thinking and shape ideas. Use of visual strategies helps link ideas, eliminate repetition, and facilitate memory.
   • Cards and affinity charts. Affinity charts are a way to gather diverse ideas and begin clustering them so each cluster can be addressed. It is a way of going from whole to part.

An example of an affinity process is as follows: Have each person write one idea on a card. Post the cards on a white board or flip chart.

Discover the four or five main ideas, or headings, that organize the thoughts. Limit the number of main headings to four or five, because more than that is counterproductive. Write those headings across the top of pieces of paper or on the white board, and then put the cards under the appropriate headings to see the intensity of some of the ideas.

After gathering the ideas, it is the task of the facilitator to guide the process to look at other key questions. Of these ideas, what does the group have control of? What is out of their control? What items are relatively short-term interventions? Which interventions can only occur over time?

For example, the fifth-grade team was looking at math scores that were lower than desired on the statewide math assessment. People wrote ideas—one per card. The facilitator then analyzed the data and derived four major headings: curriculum, instruction, parental support, scheduling. The cards were then put into columns by topic.

By clustering the ideas, participants can readily see which ideas have the most immediacy or potency.

The next step was to look at the ideas generated under each heading and then ask those key questions—What does the group have

Issue: Low Test Scores on Fifth-Grade Math Test

Instruction	Curriculum	Scheduling	Parental Support

control of? What is out of their control? What items are relatively short-term interventions? Which interventions can only occur over time? For scheduling, for example, one of the ideas was to use some of the flextime in the day so students can get more math instruction.

The group can decide how to proceed. They can remove the items that are out of their control, such as state funding, and then pick, say, one topic and work on it, such as curriculum. Or the group could develop a timeline approach. They could do some things on a short-term basis and plan for the long-term approach. The facilitator needs to assist this process, depending on the primacy of the issue, the participants involved, and the resources that can be devoted to the topic.

Another approach would be to divide the group into four subgroups so that each subgroup decides what could happen under each of the four topics. They would have to answer the same questions about control, resources, and time. The subgroups would have to decide what was realistic and establish some short- and long-term goals.

The facilitator would have to allow time for discussion and reporting out. After some possible interventions had been discussed, the group would plan for the next steps. It may be that the group wants to approach one topic at a time or take the most immediate topic and begin by urgency.

Over time the group can come back to the original chart to keep track of the progress that has been made and to help establish future goals. The chart can be a living document that can be presented to an entire staff or even a parent group.

- Use trigger words (Garmston & Wellman, 1999, p. 199). In brainstorming situations we sometimes get stuck because the same ideas appear over and over: "If we had more money, more time, more parental involvement," for example. Although those are valid concerns, they also can be excuses that are roadblocks to other ideas.

So how can we get beyond the same old responses? One way is to use what Garmston and Wellman call *trigger words*. (This is a strategy gifted/talented teachers have known for a long time. Marketing majors also recognize it as a strategy to think outside the box. In his book, *Whack on the Side of the Head*, Roger van Oech [1998] used it as a strategy in business meetings to get people to think differently.) Examples of trigger words are *magnify, minimize, rearrange, combine, adapt, reverse*.

How would one use trigger words? In the previous example of the fifth-grade math team, for example, parents and teachers have brainstormed and clustered their ideas into the four major topics of curriculum, instruction, parental involvement, and scheduling. The facilitator would then divide the group into four subgroups and give some trigger words to each table group to see if there are ways to **magnify, minimize**, and so on, the issue of scheduling, for example. Each subgroup would then report out.

Or each subgroup could be given one trigger word that it would try to apply to all four topics. It depends on the purpose of the meeting and how much time the group has to generate ideas. Some of these decisions are shaped as the meeting progresses.

- **Force field analysis** is another common strategy for determining which items are working toward the issue and which are working against it.

Put the topic at the top of a piece of paper. "Good test scores" is a broad example. This activity can be done in table groups, as a large group, or individually. Have the participants list two columns: those things that work toward the goal and those that work against it.

The next step is to have the participants decide what can be done. It is important to get people to think about the issue from both angles because we too often get stuck when trying to take away the things that work against the goal instead of spending more time generating those forces that work toward it. Some of the forces toward the goal may actually be self-extinguishing for those that work against it.

When looking at both columns it is again important for the group to question what it has control over. What is beyond its control or

Forces for Good Test Scores	Forces Against Good Test Scores
$\longrightarrow$	$\longleftarrow$

purview? What are interventions that the group can actually achieve? It does no good to rail against No Child Left Behind, for example, if there is nothing that the group can do. Instead, the leader must facilitate the energies toward ideas that can be accomplished and can make a difference, like providing more direct instruction, changing schedules, or adding specific supplemental materials to cover weak areas.

- **Fishbone diagrams**. Fishbone diagrams are visual strategies to help categorize brainstormed ideas into topics that can be addressed individually. It is a way to see the positives and negatives side-by-side.

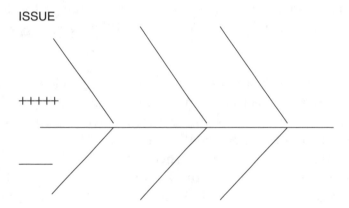

If the issue is still the fifth-grade math, each topic (e.g., curriculum, scheduling) is a "bone." The pluses can be listed on the top half of the page and the negatives on the bottom half to see the positive forces of curriculum, for example. Is there a way that these positives can be strengthened?

What are the negatives? How can they be ameliorated? Again, the group must decide on its approach and which items can be worked on as a start.

Many other strategies exist for facilitators. However, the ones that we need the most are strategies to move a discussion, to present ideas visually, and then move on.

Types of Decision-Making

Depending on the charge of the group, the leader needs to know what type of decision-making will be practiced in the group: consensus, voting with majority making the choice, or by command decision.

Consensus

Consensus decisions are used when all members of the team agree to support the group's decision both publicly and privately, even if the selected option is not their first choice. Each member is able to "live with" the decision. A leader would use consensus-building and decision-making when:

- People are able to have extensive dialog and express their opinions.
- Full support and commitment are needed in order to implement the decision successfully.
- The decision affects or may change the core process of those involved.

We tend to use the term *consensus-building* loosely, and some leaders believe they have a consensus when they actually have a majority vote. If trying to build consensus, make certain that, at the end of the time, this question is posed to each participant: "Are you able to support the decision, privately and publicly?" If any participant says no, and the group continues as though the decision is made, then what is actually in operation is a majority vote.

Michael Fullan (1993) believes that consensus is disguised as what he describes as "collaboration [that] becomes 'groupthink'—uncritical conformity to the group, unthinking acceptance of the latest solution, suppression of individual dissent"(p. 34). He believes that "the freshest ideas often come from diversity and those marginal to the group" (p. 35). Therefore, consensus translates as a group decision that reflects the opinions of no one but is a less-than-satisfactory composite of the ideas of the whole where no one is really content.

Cuban (2001) believes the term "satisfice" is more appropriate because, in order to satisfy some need or ideas, someone must sacrifice. And "If people don't have their own vision, all they can do is 'sign up' for someone else's" (Fullan, 1993, p. 29).

Consensus takes time and a skilled facilitator to address the concerns of all in the group. A jury vote in a capital case is usually a consensus vote where all agree to the outcome. However, sometimes it is a "hung jury" because not everyone can "satisfice" their beliefs to agree to the will of the majority. If members of a group are silent, and everyone else says they have reached consensus but the silent partner never speaks up or is called on, then it is not a consensus and the silent person has the opportunity to support or sabotage the decision.

Majority Vote

Most decisions are decided by the majority vote, particularly if the decision is made with peers. The meeting leader must decide what type of majority is necessary. What percentage makes a majority? One vote? Two-thirds of all votes?

Voting should be used when the stakes are low, the group is very large, there is not a lot of time, and commitment to the task is less important than getting on with the task.

This strategy is common and familiar to our processes. Most often curriculum adoptions are by majority vote, as are calendar decisions and decisions about which interventions to try.

Be careful in a voting situation that a "majority vote" is not confused with a "vocal vote." The old saying, "The world is run by those who show up," is a parallel to the fact that too often the world is run by those who SPEAK up. Be sure to get all opinions into the room so they can be discussed. Do not let the domineering, more vocal ones get their votes to count more than the silent thinkers'.

Doing silent ballots will help get a more honest vote, for example. Or a thumbs up, down, or sideways vote can give a hint as to the mood of the whole group and not everyone can see all the votes at once.

Command Decision

A command decision is made by the person with the positional authority or charge to do so. Such decisions are usually made in groups with participants who have unequal power. For example, some districts use committees to interview possible principal candidates. Members of the staff, the community, and even students may be on the interview committee. They listen and may rank the candidates, but the ultimate decision, the command decision, is made by the superintendent.

Command decision may be used when:

- The group does not have the expertise or authority to make such a decision.
- Relatively quick action is needed.
- It is the law.
- The decision is consistent with an already defined plan of action.
- There is little room for other options.
- The leader is willing to accept full responsibility for the consequences of the decision.
- The group agrees to allow one individual to make the decision.

Hints for Running Productive, Successful Meetings

Managing the Agenda

After all the preparation work, it is time for the meeting. The first item is to make certain that everyone has been **introduced**. Next, conduct **housekeeping items**. If necessary, let people know the locations of the bathrooms and soda machines. Then review the timing of the meeting, when breaks and lunch will be, if the meeting is long, and the time of closure.

(A tool for the facilitator is to have an agenda with the approximate length of **time that will be devoted to each item listed on the right-hand** side. The facilitator can watch the agenda and the clock to make certain that all necessary items are covered well and important topics are not short-changed, and, conversely, that small items do not take more time than warranted.)

Take notes. It is helpful to prepare one agenda with lots of white space after each item so notes can be taken right on the agenda and then typed shortly thereafter. It is more efficient to use technology, if possible, such as a laptop, a palm pilot with keyboard, or a SmartBoard, to take notes that would only need to be downloaded or uploaded, edited, and dispersed. The agenda can be preloaded and notes taken directly on it.

Appoint a recorder, if possible. It is difficult to lead a meeting and take notes at the same time. But if there is no one who can take notes, then use key words and phrases as mnemonic devices rather than writing complete sentences. Be sure to include enough information so that the notes are accurate. If someone else is the recorder, be sure the handwriting is legible.

Address **one topic at a time**. If the conversation starts to veer toward another topic, it is the job of the facilitator to bring the topic back to the idea under discussion.

Any meeting that lasts over one and a half hours needs to have a **scheduled break**. It seems that attention spans for adults are less than for students. Studies have shown that in an hour-long class or session, for example, the first and last 10 minutes are the most memorable. Because there is a decrease in attention in the middle, it is important to schedule activities that necessitate movement, discussion, or other active involvement during that time. Therefore, for an hour and a half meeting, the first 10–15 minutes and last 10–15 minutes are what people will remember most. Use these times to set the tone and then to provide closure.

Always **provide closure;** sum up the accomplishments of the meeting. Providing such an activity gives the participants an opportunity to clarify ideas and insures that everyone feels they attended the same meeting. Closure gives participants common language, particularly if they are to report back to someone, such as their staff or grade-level team.

Some strategies of closure are

- **Recall**—Recall what happened in the meeting. Refer to the goal of the meeting and demonstrate how it was accomplished.
- **Rehearse**—Rehearse the decisions that were made as an outcome. For example, if it is the committee to decide the next year's calendar, repeat the reasons that certain decisions were made so that the participants can convey information accurately to their various staffs.
- **Pose a possible task** for the next meeting, if necessary. Recall the goal for the day; rehearse what happened, and then set an idea or tone for what needs to happen at the next meeting.

Provide refreshments, particularly **water**. Water is very important for people to be able to concentrate. More and more people drink bottled water. This may be a difference in generational style, but fewer people are drinking coffee, particularly after lunch. If coffee is provided for an afternoon or evening meeting, it should be decaffeinated, or at least a choice should be offered. In addition, there are more people drinking sodas in the morning. Cold weather may warrant hot beverages; and during hot weather, iced tea is often a welcome change.

If the meetings last more than one and a half hours, **provide snacks**. Snacks for midmorning and midafternoon breaks are deeply appreciated. More people appreciate fresh fruit or even popcorn in the afternoon. That being said, chocolate is always a favorite. Another good option is some type of hard candy for people to suck on, particularly in the afternoons. The "Jolly Rancher" brand of candies is a favorite, but mints rarely get chosen.

Begin on time and end a few minutes early. Participants always like the gift of time, particularly if they feel they have been efficient and gotten their task done early. In addition, it makes it appear as though the facilitator was effective and ran a good meeting.

Provide **minutes** of the meeting electronically if possible within 24 hours after the meeting. Again, that makes people impressed with the efficiency and competence, and it reinforces that what they did was important enough to get prompt feedback.

Make certain the room is pleasant. Fresh flowers in the room go far in providing the feeling that people are valued. If possible, and if the meetings last for a couple of days, it is nice to have some **small token** that the participants can take back with them after the meeting. There are many companies that provide catalogs for such tokens—such as a highlighter, a pen, a pad of post-its. However, do not do this if it would be perceived as a frivolous expenditure in a time of strained finances.

Pay attention to **voice intonation**. Statements that are declarative sentences with the voice dropping at the end are seen as credible and knowledgeable. "Let's begin the meeting" (voice going down).

If the voice is raised at the end of the sentence, the message is questioning, less definite. It suggests uncertainty or the solicitation of information. Many women use questioning styles unconsciously, particularly in a largely male-dominated meeting, so they are not per-ceived as overpowering. It is a way to suggest an opinion without stat-ing it overtly. "Is it possible that we need a new attendance policy?" has a very different flavor than "We need a new attendance policy."

Hidden Agendas

Meetings may get "sandbagged" if the participants come with and act on hidden individual or group agendas. It is an incredible responsibility of the facilitator to find out if those agendas exist and, if they do, to decide whether to air them in a respectful, productive manner or to restructure the meeting.

For example, there is a meeting to talk about designing next year's school calendar. There are representatives from each building present to put it together. Some of the representatives were appointed and some volunteered. Yet, some people are on the committee to make certain that there is a two-week winter break. Others are on the committee because they want to be out as early as possible in the spring. However, neither of these items is spoken.

One way to try to air those agendas is to begin the meeting by ask-ing for the concerns or wishes of the group. "What would you hope to see on next year's calendar?" One person says, "A two-week win-ter break." The next says, "Out early in the spring." Another says, "A full-grade day at the end of each quarter." By doing it in a general fashion, it keeps the discussion neutral.

Next, the facilitator comes prepared with a handout for the committee about the parameters of the decision-making. Some of the parameters are the number of teacher contract days, the number of student contact days, the testing schedule, and the need to have a balanced number of days among quarters and between semesters. Then the facilitator can look at the brainstormed list and say, "To look at our list we have competing desires. Out early and a two-week break might be extinguishing needs. Therefore, can we look at our parameters and see how we can put together a calendar that works."

By laying out the wants and then describing the parameters, people can see that each person will not get their wish. By providing the facts of the calendar and the parameters, the representatives also have tools of information to use in their respective buildings to explain why the calendar is the way it is.

So how does a facilitator know if there are hidden agendas? The facilitator has given the group their charge and what their responsibility is. They begin working. Ideas are brought forward, but it feels like there is always a "yes, but . . ." There may be hidden agendas working to subvert the process.

As another example, a group has gathered to discuss how to implement world language in the middle level. Each time a possible scheduling option appears, someone, particularly a certain someone or group, establishes a "yes, but . . ." If it feels like the discussion cannot move forward no matter what option is proposed, there may be a hidden agenda. In this case, it may be that some of the participants teach a different elective that may be cut if world language is added.

It is helpful to understand the culture of the organization or building in order to better understand and deal with some of the hidden agendas. It is also helpful to know the players in the room. If possible, gather some background data prior to the meeting.

One way of dealing with hidden agendas is to think of rephrasing the "yes, but . . ." into "yes, **and**." Is there a way to have world language and not decrease other electives? Or does someone have to bite the bullet and say that this is the way the district is going because it represents sound educational decisions? If so, that too will have to be stated and explained so people in the meeting can go away and explain it to their peers.

Knowing Yourself

Good facilitators or meeting leaders must be self-aware. Good meeting leaders act as catalysts for the process and may choose to enter into the discussion when appropriate but still must maintain the responsibility to the process of conducting a productive meeting. To do this, leaders must:

- Know their **personal strengths and weaknesses**. Is your philosophy in opposition to some of the members of the group?

If it is, and you are the facilitator, you may need to keep your personal beliefs out of the discussion. It is the task of the group to accomplish a goal, and the facilitator may have to concentrate on the process and not be vested in the outcome.

- Understand their personal "**hot buttons.**" If certain beliefs arouse strong feelings in facilitators, they need to know that and watch so that the meetings are not swayed to match the beliefs of the facilitators at the expense of the needs of the meetings.

The previous story about the calendar meeting is a good example. When the parents on the committee keep pushing for a certain week in March for spring break because that is the week they have booked their condos, this is a hot button for the facilitator who believes that vacations are not a good reason for determining breaks on a school calendar. The facilitator needs to come back to the calendar parameters. The facilitator should not appear annoyed or disparaging of the comment because every person has a viewpoint. It may work out in deciding the number of days among the quarters that the spring break works out at the time the parents wanted it, and it may not. But by using the process, it does not become personal.

- Be aware of **body language**, both of self and of others. Are you signaling engagement or disengagement? Are you leaning forward toward the table and showing involvement, or is your chair pushed back and you are away from the table with your arms crossed, which appears more separate? Are you looking out the window, which may seem to signal a lack of investment, or are you making eye contact as people speak? Are you doodling and looking down, which may seem disinterested, or are you looking at participants?
- Have various **tools** for keeping the group focused. Watch the time. Monitor the agenda. Are important topics getting enough time? Use interventions to keep the group moving. Is the discussion on topic?
- **Care about the people** in the group. It is important to build relationships and trust with the people of the group. If the facilitator cares and demonstrates that by tone of voice, engagement, and skills, the group is more likely to go forward and be satisfied with the outcome of the meeting, even if the outcome is not what they wanted personally. If the group does not trust the facilitator or perceives that the facilitator does not care about them, it is easy to blame the outcome of the meeting on

the facilitator and sabotage the outcome of the meeting. Trust builds loyalty to the process and to the outcome.

Conflict in Meetings

Conflict is a part of human interactions. An excellent resource on conflict in general is *Getting Past No: Negotiating With Difficult People* (1991) by William Ury. Meetings are a good place to bring out and resolve conflict because people are brought together to discuss, learn, solve problems, and, in general, make good decisions. Fullan (1993) says, "Conflict is a necessary part of change" (p. 62). Conflict comes from problems and "Problems are inevitable, but the good news is that you can't learn or be successful without them" (p. 25).

Fullan believes that conflict creates energy, which then spurs us forward. A hurricane is a good example because it causes natural conflict, disruption, and devastation, but, on a positive note, it also helps diffuse global warming. With humans, conflict can also cause disruption in addition to doing away with some old ideas and helping people to get unstuck.

However, educators may find it difficult to disagree, especially openly. Some people avoid disagreements by not voicing their true opinions in meetings but wait until side conversations in the parking lot to discuss what they REALLY think.

Healthy organizations and healthy meetings are ones in which the participants are able to express respectful conflicts and disagreements and still work together for a common good. It is healthy to realize that, although opinions may not change, they can be put aside for the good of the students.

Here are some strategies to use if conflict arises in a meeting.

- **Restate the goal of the meeting**. If the conflict is about a side topic, and could be intended to derail the conversation or to vent some personal frustration on the part of a participant, bring the discussion back to the topic of the meeting. Interrupt the flow of the argument by referring to the topic of the day. Do not let arguments proceed to the point of no reconciliation. Do not let the conflict become personal.

An example is a grade-level team meeting. The purpose of the meeting is to discuss upcoming field trips. However, one person is angry with the principal and starts venting about it. The meeting leader needs to cut it short, in a respectful manner, and refresh everyone's memory as to the purpose of the day.

- **Take time out**. Interrupt the discussion and call for a break. During the break talk to the parties concerned. If the conflict is between two people, it may be time to suggest another person to act as a disinterested third-person mediator.

For example, a meeting was held to talk about purchasing new books for a certain department. For some unknown reason two people became heavily invested in using the opportunity to vent about how they felt the administration was not supporting them and that the administration needs to be concerned primarily with the health of their teachers. That was not the topic of the meeting. One strategy was to call a break and discuss privately with the teachers what can be done about their concerns.

- **Honor the conflict but suggest dealing with it at a different time and/or with different people**. Depending on the depth of the disagreement and the pervasiveness of the conflict, the leader can either deal with the conflict as a group right then and there or honor the concerns of the group. "I hear your concern about. . . . However, this is not the time for that discussion. I (or someone more appropriate) would be willing to help facilitate a discussion about that topic at another meeting. We also need some other key players to be part of that discussion. If people want to do that, let's strategize about that after this meeting. Are people okay with that? Can we move back to today's topic and we'll meet at 3:30 to discuss the other part." By honoring people's feelings, you signal to the group that you care, that their concerns are powerful. By agreeing to help facilitate another meeting, you also may be able to bring more appropriate people into the room.
- **Listen actively and paraphrase for corrections.** If the conflict is between two people, or two ideas, ask each of the opponents to listen to the other's point of view and then paraphrase it to make certain that the sender's message is the same as the received message. If the conflict is something pertinent to the group, brainstorm possible solutions and ideas to solve it. As a leader you may be able to point out areas where both agree. You may want to do a force field analysis by listing the two viewpoints and then finding the commonalities. Narrow the discussion down to the real issue and then try to brainstorm possible solutions.
- **Use the "broken record" technique**. Sometimes people want to vent without regard to the purpose of the meeting. If, as leader,

one has intervened by trying to bring the topic back to the point of the day, and someone tries again to derail this, repeat, "The purpose of today is . . ." One may need to do this several times in the meeting. Keep the voice cordial, but firm. Do not get into the emotionality of it.

- **It is not about you**. Know your hot buttons. If this is a topic that is potent for you, remember that you are leading the meeting and must monitor the process. It is about getting the work done.
- **Reframe the disagreement**. Participants in a meeting often want the leader to suggest the solution. Sometimes that is because the leader may have more expertise; other times it could be because if the leader makes the choice, then the participants are "off the hook" and have someone to blame if things do not go the way they want. Decide as facilitator which is appropriate. Whose issue is it? Does it need your expertise? Or are you the fall guy for adults who do not want to act like adults and they can just blame you?

Reframing is to ask, "What do you suggest?" "If you could wave a magic wand, how would you solve this?" "In a perfect world, how would this look?"

One of the values of reframing is to get people to think differently and get unstuck. It is also to get people to look at their own behavior and values. Also, as an administrator, it is important to keep the problem where it belongs. Teachers, parents, and students all want to dump their problems on someone else, which is neither appropriate nor healthy. Redirecting the questions to the questioner makes them responsible for generating a possible solution.

An example is when there is unprofessional behavior occurring among a department staff that is creating an unhealthy, unproductive work environment. In addition, people are being mean and hurtful by their gossip. The principal has met with the individuals, but nothing has changed. Performance goals have been drafted, but the behavior remains. Finally, the leader plans a meeting to deal with the conflict in a group setting so that all participants have the same information, they cannot use "divide and conquer" by forming unholy alliances with individuals, and they cannot use misinformation to keep the conflict alive.

On the surface the conflict appears to be about job responsibilities. However, the underlying issue is about jealousy among various department members. They do not want to own their bad behavior and want to be upset with everyone else and use blame to create discontent within the department.

Before the meeting the leader should plan the surroundings. The leader should sit at the head of the table and contrive it so the other participants are sitting facing each other and in front of the facilitator. The leader should set a time for the meeting when other administrators can be in the room as witnesses and recorders. The other administrators should be alerted ahead of time about the purpose of the meeting and the strategy involved.

The meeting starts with the leader laying the groundwork of the history and reason for the meeting. "There has been unprofessional behavior and gossip. There are hard feelings because some people perceive they are being asked to do things outside their job description and it is perceived that others are getting off easier. It seems as though the climate has not changed even though there have been private conversations and goal-setting opportunities with individuals."

"I have tried to resolve the conflict. It has not worked. Maybe we have not defined the issue adequately." Then each person is asked for their understanding of the issues. Write them down in a visible spot—white board, flip chart, and so on—as people share.

Then reframe. "Is it fair to say that the issue is. . .?" When people agree on the issue, put the responsibility back where it belongs—with those who are choosing to continue their bad behavior. Ask, "What do you suggest at this point? I will ask each one of you what it is that you need and what you can do to remedy the problem."

There are two issues here: what each person needs and what each will do to remedy the situation. Make two lists, one of needs and the other of solutions. Develop some strategies to address what people need. Then ask each person what they can do as a solution. If the situation is severe, the facilitator can even develop written contracts and have the individuals sign them. At the end of the meeting provide closure by restating the understanding of what will happen from then on.

If, however, the contracts or conversations do not work, then it is time to work with the human resources department to develop improvement plans. At this point the teachers may want to have their union representatives available.

- **Disarm the conflict**. One way to disarm the conflict is by a simple "Thank you." "Thank you for bringing that issue to the table. Let's discuss it. . . ." Or "Can we discuss this when so-and-so is here?" Or "Can we talk about this after the meeting because our topic today is. . . ?" Do the unexpected by acknowledging the conflict as legitimate. By doing so, the power of the disruption is removed.

- **Involve the nay-sayers**. If someone brings up a point of conflict, ask if they would be willing to spearhead a task force to investigate and come up with a solution. A member of the team will always have a criticism or a better idea. Put that person in charge of preparing a report on the topic for the next meeting. Ask if there is anyone else who would like to help him, therefore giving him some support as well. The idea may even produce some very creative solutions.

- **Create forced-choice situations that are win/win for the meeting**. "If we continue this discussion, we will not have time to . . ." "We can either talk about it in a separate meeting or you can bring it up at a staff meeting." (Either option is a good one, but note that neither choice involves continuing the discussion that day because it is not on topic.) "Which would you prefer . . .?" Provide two good options, let them pick, and either way it is a win/win for the facilitator and the participants.

Training/Coaching Meetings

Another type of meetings for educational leaders is training and coaching sessions. Many of the other meeting strategies apply to these as well, such as how to set an agenda, facilitation skills, how to manage a meeting, and how to manage conflict. In addition, there are some other necessary considerations.

Some Practical Hints for Conducting Training Sessions

- Be very clear about the **necessary outcomes** of the session. Have them posted or at the top of the agenda. Have no more than three major outcomes.

- Know **who** is being trained. Are the participants experienced in this area or are they novices? Is there a mixture of the two? Are people there voluntarily or is this mandated? Are people being paid to be there? What is the expectation for the participants after the training? Will they be seen as training the trainers? Will they be expected to perform certain tasks? What is their accountability? Who will monitor that?

- Provide an **agenda** for the participants and list what the **outcomes** will be. "By the end of the training, you will be able to. . . ." After today, it is expected that you will. . . ." "So-and-so will be in charge of making this initiative happen, so if you have questions, defer them to. . . ." **Close the meeting** by repeating the outcomes. "I told you at the beginning that you will be able to . . . and you are doing. . . ." Be sure you do a recap and provide the full circle. Providing a recap also helps people to remember how far they have come.

If it is a daylong training, provide a **recap of the morning before the participants** break for lunch, and then do it again in the afternoon. People have a tendency to forget what happens in the morning.

A very helpful **feedback tool** for trainers, particularly if the training lasts more than one day, is to use blank manila folders as feedback sheets. Put one participant's name on each tab. If it is a two-day session, use the first half above the fold for the first day and the bottom half for the second. At the end of each day, ask for feedback for half of the space. The bottom half of the space will be for the leader to write comments. Then in the morning, the leader returns the folder to the participants.

On the second day you can use the section below the fold in the same manner. The participant writes on half and the facilitator writes on the other half. Taking time to write back to participants is invaluable. The trainer gets timely information from each person. Because it is private, the participant can be frank, sometimes brutally so, but that is rare. Mostly it is helpful to get a good feel about the group. It is also a good way for participants to ask private questions that they fear others already know the answers to.

Summary

It is important to run good meetings. Because meetings are a process, there are several process questions to ask before a meeting begins.

What type of meeting is it—with those less knowledgeable than me, with peers, with superiors, with a diverse group?

How long is it? One to one and a half hours, a half day, one day or more?

What materials do I need?

How will I arrange the physical surroundings?

What is the charge of the meeting?

Who makes the decision? What kind of decision-making process will I use—consensus, voting, command?

In addition, it is important to know of any hidden agendas that the participants may have because it will help the leader to be prepared for any underlying conflict that may erupt into open conflict at the meeting.

Know yourself and keep YOU out of the meetings.

Understand group dynamics and group processes.

Have some processing skills at your fingertips for brainstorming, resolving conflict, and reaching a decision.

Most important, run the meeting. Start on time and end early, and have a work product so that the participants can feel good about their participation.

Meetings are like the description of life by Samuel Butler:

"[Meetings] Life is like playing a violin in public and learning the instrument as one goes on."

Personal Journal

1. Do I run meetings or do I just let them happen?

2. What facilitation skills do I need to practice?

3. How well do I encourage and resolve conflict?

Group Discussion

1. How is the management of meetings a powerful educational leadership tool?

2. Keep a log of different types of meetings that happen on a weekly basis. As an effective manager/educational leader, do I structure them according to need, participant, or task, or do I just let them happen? How can I be more effective in my leadership/management style?

11

Accountability as Opera

Accountability is one of those contemporary buzzwords that are very emotionally laden. Because it has been associated with certain political agendas, administrators may actually have a physical response when they hear the word. However, accountability is a current fact of life in public education.

Accountability is much like an opera, consisting of main actors, supporting actors, and a chorus that sings arias, duets, and choruses. There is a story line—sometimes fraught with emotion—and intricacies that contribute to the plot. There are complex interactions and subplots for the story line and musical overlays that provide interpretation to the words. There are separate acts with an intermission to give time to pause. There is a resolution to the episode, but the plot continues. In addition, the scenery, colors, and lighting all provide a depth and richness that can add or detract from the action on stage.

Accountability, too, has many actors—teachers, parents, administrators, politicians, community members, and, of course, students. The story line also contains many components—curriculum, professional development, assessments, and community involvement. There are arias, duets, and choral numbers, because sometimes people work alone, sometimes they work in tandem, and sometimes everyone sings and works together. Often there is interplay from a person to a duet to a chorus and then back.

In addition, the plot contains many intricacies. Although it is divided into "acts," yearly segments of measuring progress (there's even a summer intermission), the episode comes to a halt at the end of the year, but the story line continues. The overlay of community, socioeconomics, settings, and so on, provide the staging that can make the experience pleasing or painful.

The role of an instructional leader in this opera is twofold: First, the leader must be the director, the person who brings all the pieces together, by finding funding, managing the location, choosing the plot, choosing the actors, rehearsing, modifying the action, setting the stage, and all the other pieces that a director does to stage a major enterprise. The director works hard in front, behind the scenes, and around the scenes but during the actual performance is of minimal importance.

Second, the leader is the conductor who directs the orchestra and the actors on stage, who may poke his or her head out of the pit once in a while to greet the crowd and then duck back down to get back to business.

Plot-building elements of this opera are items such as curriculum, professional development, and external constituents, which were discussed in previous chapters. This chapter will deal with the other elements, such as the concept of accountability, key elements of data collection, management, and holistic accountability.

Accountability

The current enactment of the Elementary and Secondary Education Act (ESEA), commonly called No Child Left Behind (NCLB), was put into law in January of 2002. Since 1965 the federal government has passed an education act that delineates its involvement in public education. This recent enactment changed the focus in that it proscribes that all students will be proficient in reading, math, and science by 2014.

Since 1993 states have had to develop academic standards for all students. Now states are to test against those standards to define proficiency. All schools must be increasing their numbers of proficient students to reach 100% by 2014. Another component of the law is that each state must publicize information about the progress of each school and each district in a manner that is easily understood by parents. On the basis of that information and whether schools make adequate yearly progress (AYP), parents may opt to send their child(ren) to other schools.

The law also states that students have to be taught by highly qualified teachers who are licensed to teach in the areas in which they are providing instruction. Paraprofessionals must also be highly qualified.

The federal law is under constant scrutiny and is always being "tweaked" as states become more involved in this process over time. However, most believe that the basic elements of assessing progress, publishing data for community perusal, and requiring highly qualified teachers and paraprofessionals will remain constants in the accountability recipes.

Leader's Role as Opera Director

The opera director, or educational leader, is in charge of the entire operation by defining the goals, marshalling resources, and making certain it happens. Certain elements of that role have been defined previously with the role in curriculum, professional development, working with external constituents, and so on.

As opera director for accountability, the instructional leader needs to understand the legal facets of the laws, both federal and state. An excellent resource is the federal government's education Web site (http://www.ed.gov). It is also important to use individual state department of education Web sites for local information, because states are allowed to have unique plans to meet the requirements of the federal law.

In addition, the leader must understand data-driven leadership, data-driven decision-making, assessment and its many facets, and holistic accountability.

Data-Driven Leadership

It is the task of the instructional leader to facilitate the accountability process by using what Scott McLeod, the project director of the School Technology Leadership Initiative, called "data-driven leadership." Data-driven leadership is results-driven, practice-oriented, aligned, caring, rooted in good research and theory, and flexible (McLeod, 2004). He described nine components of data-driven leadership: 1) a solid understanding of data-driven decision-making principles; 2) multifaceted data collection; 3) SMART goal setting; 4) faster feedback cycles; 5) professional learning communities that are rooted in information; 6) data transparency; 7) data safety;

8) adequate technological infrastructure; and 9) resources on the ultimate goal of student achievement (McLeod, 2004).

First, a leader needs a solid understanding of **data-driven decision-making principles**. If a leader feels that this is an area of little or no training, there are many books and training programs available currently for self-study. Victoria Bernhardt's (1998) *Data Analysis for Comprehensive Schoolwide Improvement* is one approach. The North Central Regional Educational Laboratory has tools to use that are accessible through their Web site (http://www.ncrel.org). The April 2001 issue of *The School Administrator*, published by the American Association of School Administrators, is devoted to data-driven decisions. Mike Schmoker has written many articles and books on the process, one of which is *The Results Fieldbook: Practical Strategies From Dramatically Improved Schools*, published by ASCD in 2001.

In addition, there are many good conferences to attend. Ideally, there is a data/evaluation person within the district who can assume the leadership as an in-house resource and expert. What is important is that the leader find a system that makes sense for the particular site and then use it to develop common terminology with a staff.

Second, the **collection of data should be multifaceted**. To get a complete picture, it is necessary to gather multiple measures of progress with multiple indicators. For example, Bernhardt (1998) describes the multiple measures as demographics, perceptions, student learning, and school processes.

An example of multiple indicators is standardized testing and formative assessments. The types of data to use is the source of in-depth study for an administrator and too lengthy to describe fully here. But as one becomes involved in the data-driven leadership process, leaders will need to gain a richer understanding of all the possibilities.

Third, SMART (specific, measurable, attainable, relevant, and trackable) goal setting should be standard practice. Goals need to be

Specific—Improve reading scores

Measurable—Improve reading scores by 5 points

Attainable—It is not attainable to improve all students by two grade levels, for example

Relevant—Goals pertain to academic achievement (an irrelevant goal to academic achievement would be to "build a new school sign")

Trackable—It is important to be able to measure progress toward a goal.

"Improving school climate" is a good example of an untrackable goal unless attainable steps are embedded into the goal, such as "improve school climate as measured by increased attendance at parent conferences from 75% to 85% attendance by parents."

One of the biggest problems with goals when people write them for personal growth plans or for site plans is that they are not SMART: "Build knowledge and implementation strategies for differentiating instruction." "Continue efforts in the development and use of effective teaching strategies for diverse learners." "Build the community by building relational trust among students, staff, and administration to promote student achievement." All of these are wonderful goals, but where is the measurability? How do we know if they are attained? Where is the specificity? How do we track them?

Fourth, feedback cycles need to be faster. Using annual test scores to shape instruction is not enough. Teachers need to use formative assessments and other indicators on an ongoing basis so that instruction can be enhanced, redirected, retaught, or modified on a fluid basis.

Fifth, practicing professional learning communities must be established. To do that, data must be available and usable. In a previous chapter we discussed the importance of professional development in its contribution to a professional learning community. It is important that people have adequate information to make appropriate decisions.

Sixth, data should be open to practitioners. Fifth-grade teachers should be able to see third-grade data. High school English teachers should be able to see social studies data. The community should be able to see data. Although there are data privacy issues, teams can still use classroom data without using student names.

Seventh, using data to improve instruction is important, but data should not be used as an evaluative tool. Mr. Li's classroom has higher test scores than Ms. Smith's; therefore, he is a "better teacher and should get a raise" is a fear of teachers as to how data will be used. Instead, in the spirit of a professional learning community, if one class has better scores than another, then the team starts asking probing questions to find out why, so that the success can be replicated. How did Mr. Li teach the unit? What are the reading scores of the students involved? Is Mr. Li's class filled with better readers?

Eighth, there must be adequate technological infrastructure. Some districts are able to purchase data warehousing systems that can help teachers store, retrieve, and utilize data. They are able to ask probing questions and use drill-down procedures to discover root causes (McLeod, 2004).

Some districts have assessment directors who are able to understand data and provide professional development for staff. Some people are skilled with spreadsheets, so they can use technological tools to make sense of data. It is important throughout this process to build the skills of the staff in looking at data, in using technology tools, in questioning techniques, and in making valid assessments.

Finally, the leader aligns resources on the ultimate goal of student achievement. The leader must work to have curriculum alignment and professional development, as described previously. The leader must also make certain that the staff understands assessments, both formative and summative, and the difference between assessment and testing, which will be discussed next.

The leader must help to set aside time for professional discussions to occur. The leader must gather human and inanimate resources together to allow the process to occur. The leader must keep the central focus on student achievement. As Stephen Covey (1994), in his book *First Things First*, said, we have to "Keep the Main thing, the Main Thing" (p. 75), and in this situation the main thing is student achievement.

Assessment

A key feature of the data process is to understand assessment. There are assessments at the state, local, and classroom levels (Carr & Harris, 2001, p. 62). The state has its own assessments that measure progress toward proficiency against the standards. Locally, a district may have other assessments that measure progress toward the district's own curriculum, such as the assessments designed by the Northwest Evaluation Association (NWEA). There are also standardized assessments, such as those of the NAEP, that are used to compare states across the nation.

In addition, teachers use classroom assessments to measure progress against the learning goals and essential questions of the teacher. All of these are important, but the crucial ones are those of the teacher. It is on this foundation that the others are built. Douglas Reeves (2004) stated a "cardinal principle of measurement: it is more important and accurate to measure a few things frequently and consistently than to measure many things once" (p. 25). As a leader, how can you use this statement? The instructional leader needs to make certain that teachers understand the purpose of assessment, how to design valid assessments, and how to use assessment to guide instruction.

Having common assessments for common courses is an important tool in improving student progress. For example, all ninth-grade students have to take civics. The ninth-grade teachers design a common assessment. What creates learning and builds achievement is when teachers are able to get together to look at the results of this assessment to see how the students did and why. As an outgrowth, the teachers are then able to learn from each other how to teach certain concepts. Also, teachers are able to define what professional development is necessary for certain people in order to help students learn. Having such an atmosphere is a professional learning community. It is the creation of such a community that is the task of an instructional leader.

Within the process of creating a learning community, teachers must understand formative and summative assessments. Summative assessments are used to see what a student has learned as an end point. For example, ACTs and final exams are summative.

Formative assessments are those used to help shape instruction-in-process. Running records for reading, exit cards for a day's lesson, thumbs up or down to answer a question—all are formative, so teachers can get a sense of who knows what. If all students understand, then the teacher can move on. If not, the teacher must reteach to those who do not have the concepts mastered.

Holistic Accountability

Doug Reeves, the author of *Accountability for Learning: How Teachers and School Leaders Can Take Charge* (2004), talked about "holistic accountability" as a way to look at accountability from a student-centered approach that "includes a balance of quantitative and qualitative indicators—the story behind the numbers . . . in a system that includes specific information on curriculum, teaching practices, and leadership practices" (p. 6).

A leader creates the opportunity for holistic accountability as "more constructive. . . . because it focuses on the improvement of teaching and learning rather than merely rendering an evaluation and publication of a report" (p. 88). The elements of holistic accountability are student achievement data, standards and curriculum, teaching strategies and professional practice, and *accountability for leaders and policy makers* [emphasis mine] (Reeves, 2002, p. 6).

What makes holistic accountability different is the use of qualitative data, accountability for leaders and policy makers, and the use of the question "Can the stakeholders use this information productively?" (p. 12). Reeves believes that data should be meaningful and, if it is of no use, then it should not be reported and recorded. For example, on one state's report card, as part of the accountability system, the salary information of school board members are collected and reported. I know of no study of direct or indirect correlation of school board salaries and student achievement.

The important pieces for this discussion are the consequences for leadership in accountability. Reeves (2004) described several roles for system leaders. The first is, leaders must catch teachers doing something right.

Second, they must provide focus. Not only must leaders help describe the vision and help maintain focus on student achievement, they also must provide modeling and time for what Reeves calls "weeding the garden." He believes that educators suffer from "initiative fatigue," where "each additional initiative, program, task, or swell idea results in fewer minutes of time, fewer dollars, and generally less leadership attention and emotional energy of teachers to make each successive initiative work" (2004, p. 59). To prevent the fatigue, teachers and administrators alike must "weed the garden," remove items that are no longer viable, are merely pro forma, are irrelevant, and so on. Administrators must model this behavior. Are there meetings that are traditional but accomplish nothing? Could the same information be given through email? Are there standing committees that need to sit down because they no longer serve a purpose? Are there reports that are redundant?

Part of the task of the administrator is to say no to ideas that do not fit the mission of student achievement. If it does not relate to the mission, then it is not really a good idea.

Third, the leader must redefine strategic planning. For many buildings and districts, the process of planning itself is a weed that should be pulled. A lot of time and energy are spent in meetings, drafting the vision, and defining the action steps when essentially the strategic plan has little effect on student achievement. Strategic plans look backward to establish the new goals. If we continue to look back at what we have always done, we will continue to get what we have always gotten.

What I have come to realize is that the process—the human interaction, the communication, the coming together—is what is more important. Concentrate on a future plan. What goal do you want? Define it from a SMART framework. How can it happen? How can you focus time and energy toward that goal?

Fourth, a leader needs to create holistic accountability that looks at other qualitative data—decreased drop-out rate, fewer alternative students, more inclusion of "on the bubble" students into the mainstream, more students in AP classes or classes that are taught by teachers trained in pre-AP vertical teaming strategies.

What Are Descriptors of a School That Practices Holistic Accountability?

Reeves (2004) studied schools that improved their scores and used holistic accountability. He discovered nine characteristics that the schools with the greatest academic gains had in common, which can be used as targets for instructional leaders in our current environment. Instructional leaders may want to think about how any one of the nine indicators could become part of the professional learning community within their schools.

• Impact of collaboration—Time for teacher collaboration is crucial for creating a climate that fosters job-embedded professional activities, including discussions, professional development, and action research. Faculty meetings, team planning time, district professional development days, and so on, can be structured for teams of teachers to converse over common assessments, professional development needs, instructional strategies, and inquiries into data.

• Value of feedback—Students need frequent feedback. Those schools that improve the most do not wait for report cards to give students feedback. Some schools use electronic means to tell parents where their children are on a weekly basis. Some schools give students progress reports to carry home every three weeks.

• Impact of time—Having concentrated, uninterrupted time devoted to core academic areas is absolutely vital. We know that the more time spent on task, the more students will learn.

• Action research and midcourse correction—Teachers use data to change instruction as they move through the semester without waiting for the end of the quarter or term. They conduct their own formative assessments to gather data on how students are doing. If the students are not doing as well as hoped, the teacher may change plans.

• Aligning teacher assignments with teacher preparation—It is important to have trained teachers teaching in the areas of licensure. We know that the most expert teachers should be teaching our most difficult students, regardless of whether the teacher has "earned" the right to teach only AP students. Sometimes a leader has to move a teacher to a different grade level so that the teacher's skills can be maximized. Jim Collins (2001), in his book *Good to Great,* would describe that as getting the right person in the right seat on the bus.

- Constructive data analysis—Reeves (2004) found that successful schools focused "intensively on student data from multiple sources, and they specifically focused on cohort data" (p. 70). In some states the assessments are useless, because schools have to compare this year's third graders to last year's third graders—that does not help change instruction.

- Common assessments—This is an important factor. "Schools with the greatest improvements in student achievement consistently used common assessments" (Reeves, 2004, p. 70). Assessments provide a "degree of consistency in teacher expectations that is essential if fairness is our fundamental value" (Reeves, p. 71). Common assessments validate that there are consistent expectations of all kids regardless of race, natural ability, or teacher.

- Value of every adult in the system—Holistic systems use all adults in the building. Bus drivers, custodians, and so on, are all included in professional development and have the same understanding as to the mission of the school.

- Cross-disciplinary integration—We know that as we learn, we link our learning innately to other areas. Infants do not learn in discrete subjects but constantly apply connections, sorting, and application. Little kids say the funniest things because they bring these wonderful connections to words, ideas, and concepts that adults have pigeonholed. We know that students who are musicians are better in math. We know that sometimes students can learn concepts by enacting them physically.

Role as Conductor

An opera conductor is in charge of leading the actual performance. He—and most often it is a male—pops his head out of the orchestra pit at the beginning and the end of a performance to announce that the story is about to begin or that the particular episode has concluded. He is also in charge of the tempo of the music, and therefore the storyline, throughout the performance as he directs the musicians and the actors. In addition, he makes certain that all participants receive their well-earned applause. As a conductor, the leader must make certain that there are signals of when to stop and start, and how fast to go.

Summary

Educators agree that accountability is here to stay. It is important to shape what that accountability means. It is important to be educated in the practices of using data to inform instruction. Administrators must understand how to interpret and use data, how to provide professional development to support teachers, and how to interpret data for parents.

Whether the shape of NCLB changes or not is immaterial. Educational leaders and managers must add the skill of accountability to their repertoire and not sacrifice the idea of a comprehensive public education for all students. It is truly a balancing act very similar to the Flying Wallendas in the circus.

Keeping accountability in perspective is what Thich Nhat Hanh describes as *Right Mindfulness*: "Do not lose yourself in the past. Do not lose yourself in the future. Do not get caught in your anger, worries, or fears. Come back to the present moment, and touch life deeply. This is mindfulness. We cannot be mindful of everything at the same time, so we have to choose what we find most interesting to be the object of our mindfulness" (p. 82)

Personal Journal

1. What are my strengths as a data leader?

2. Where do I need more information or training? How can I get that?

3. What resources can I use in my district?

4. What would it look like if my building had only one SMART goal?

5. What can I "weed " from my garden?

Group Discussion

1. How can we use accountability as an effective leadership or management tool?

2. What are some ways to discuss accountability with the staff so that it becomes a positive force in changing education for all students?

PART III

Reflective Skills of a 21st-Century Practitioner

12

The Gift of Mistakes

Mistakes, or missteps, or perceived mistakes, are an inherent part of leadership; they are necessary. Mistakes are actually gifts that "bring us back to the present moment" (Hanh, 1998, p. 64). Wheels do turn. Seasons must change. And mistakes happen.

Sometimes our best lessons are the events that we thought of as something that did not go well, the unsuccessful plan, the conflictual relationship, or the ineffective program. However, in examining the *why*, we discover how to change so that the plan, relationship, or program can succeed. At an even deeper level, we may actually change our perception about the issue, rather than try to change the issue itself.

An administrator conducted a day of training around the use of data to make decisions. At the end of the day the feedback forms and the comments heard in the hall after the session showed that teachers were not happy with it. "That was a waste of time." "We don't have time for this." "This isn't our job." At first the administrator was angry, and then hurt, about the comments. What he finally realized was that he had not done adequate preparation for the training. He was at a different level of awareness than the teachers. They did not see the need or the connection between his session and what they were doing in the classroom.

Therefore, he changed his way of thinking and began to lay more groundwork. Throughout the year he had team meetings, brought in test data, looked at cohorts, and started asking questions. He started giving teachers a common vocabulary around the use of data. He taught pieces of the process. He gave them time to use data, which let the teachers see how data could be used to inform their instruction.

By the end of the year the teachers were asking for more training. He changed both the process and his perception of the process.

If he had just thrown up his hands and been frustrated, he would not have redesigned the training to meet the teachers' needs. He used his mistake to reshape the session so that it became a learning experience.

What Is a Mistake?

As Westerners we are known to be linear in our thinking. We believe that time is linear, progress is linear, and that there are direct cause-and-effect relationships to almost everything, including the stock market. For example, housing starts equals a rise in the stock market. (How many houses can we build?) In education, linear thinking translates into such simplistic ideas as adopting the right reading series will automatically increase reading scores.

However, we seldom look at complex and indirect causes. What would happen if we believed that events rarely have a single cause or that problems can rarely be solved by a simple solution? What would happen if we believed as Arthur Wing Pinero did in *The Fourth Turning* by Strauss and Howe (1997) that "The future is only the past again, entered through another gate"(p. 22)?

What would it be like to think that, paraphrasing, mistakes are the event again, entered through another gate?

According to Thich Nhat Hanh (1998) in *The Heart of Buddha's Teaching*, we each have the capacity to understand things as they are. "If you plant corn, corn will grow. If you plant wheat, wheat will grow. If you act in a wholesome way, you will be happy. If you act in an unwholesome way, you water the seeds of craving, anger, and violence in yourself" (p. 52). To avoid making mistakes, it is our task to "recognize which seeds are wholesome and to encourage those seeds to be watered" (p. 52).

If we have erred, hurt someone, or made a faulty decision, we can ask ourselves some questions to help amend it.

Amending the Mistake

The first step is to recognize that something is not right, that a mistake or misstep has been made. That is not easy to do for some people. Some people never do and continue to make the same mistake over and over again.

1. Sometimes a simple, heartfelt apology is all it takes to amend a mistake. For example, if you called someone by the wrong name and you discovered the error, a simple apology goes a long way toward helping the person to realize that you know that a mistake was made and that you cared enough to amend it.

2. Sometimes "owning" the mistake is what it takes. A teacher comes to you and is critical because her team did not know about a decision that you made. Only certain people knew. You failed to communicate to everyone, so it felt to the team like there were secrets and favorite staff members. A simple statement owning the mistake is important. "I made a mistake in not calling a team meeting to discuss this with all of you at one time." It is not necessary to go overboard with the apology. In fact, apologizing too much can make the apology feel insincere.

Too often people, and administrators too, are afraid to admit an error publicly for fear of seeming incompetent, or wishy-washy, or weak. It has been my experience that people respect a sincere apology and an admission of being human. After all, we all are *very* human.

3. It is important to be honest and sincere. Some of us remember how President Carter was castigated in his famous *Playboy* interview for admitting that he "committed adultery in his heart" even though he never acted on it (http://www.arts.mcgill.ca/programs/history/faculty/TROYWEB/Courseweb/JimmyCarterThePlayboyInterview.htm). It seems that politicians find it difficult to be honest because of how it can be misconstrued, "restrued," "unstrued," or plastered across the media. However, in our school arena, it is important to be factual, honest, and open.

Owning mistakes is a way for people to move forward. In education we all have memories like elephants. We bring up events that happened 20 years ago as though they were yesterday. It is important to tell people, "That was a mistake" or " I made a mistake. Now how can we move forward?"

4. Reframe the mistake. When something bad happens, think, "What can I learn from this? How is this a gift to me?" Instead of feeling pity or depressed, one can use the experience. By reframing it, one can then reshape their behavior so that it does not happen again.

How we perceive something determines our interaction. However, "if we look more deeply, we see that *all views are wrong views*. No view can ever be the truth. It is just from one point; that is why it is called a 'point of view'" (Hanh, 1998, p. 56). Try looking at an event from the opposite point of view to see what lesson can be learned. After all, there are multiple perspectives.

Sometimes we make mistakes when we are hurrying. The mistake can be a reminder to slow down. For example, a principal received an upsetting e-mail from a teacher and quickly sat down and responded, and responded rather harshly. She later had to make amends with the teacher. It would have been prudent to wait 24 hours and then write the e-mail when her emotions were not as heightened. If she had waited, it is likely that the e-mail would not have been as curt.

Cyclical Purpose of Mistakes

Mistakes create a self-correcting cycle, like the rudder on the boat as it helps to steer a course. To a reflective leader, a mistake helps to recalculate the direction.

In addition, mistakes can give us the gift of time. In linear thinking, once an event happens, it is over. Time marches on, never to be regained. However, think of how freeing it would be to believe that time can repeat itself. If something goes awry, we can have an opportunity to correct it. I was once told that the Navajos believe that each day, each cycle of the sun, is the same day repeated over and over. If something went wrong in one cycle, then there was an opportunity in the next cycle to make it right. That is the gift mistakes give us—the opportunity to make them better.

Summary

What if you thought of a mistake as a gift? What if, as Hanh said, "No view can ever be the truth"?

Personal Journal

1. In retrospect, what was one mistake I made that turned out to be a gift?

2. What if each day were a repeat of the previous one? Would I do anything differently?

3. How could I use the ideas of restitution that we teach students with the staff?

Group Discussion

1. How can I use the idea of mistakes to be a more effective educational leader?

2. What aspects of culture would I have to change to allow people to use mistakes as a building block to further growth?

13

Knowing Yourself as a Moral and Ethical Leader

This book has offered fundamental management basics and suggestions for an instructional leader. All the management skills in the world and all the leadership training in the world will ring hollow if not combined with the deeper and richer purpose of a moral and ethical leader. But what exactly does that mean?

A moral and ethical leader must understand three things: one's own beliefs; the moral purpose of the individual; and the moral responsibility of the position of educational leader.

Personal Strengths and Beliefs

Parker Palmer (1998), in his book *The Courage to Teach*, said it so beautifully: "I am a teacher at heart, and there are moments in the classroom when I can hardly hold the joy. When my students and I discover uncharted territory to explore . . . when our experiences are illumined by the lightning-life of the mind—then teaching is the finest work I know" (p. 1). Teaching is a noble profession, one that can truly make a difference in the lives of individuals and, therefore, have a cumulative effect on ever-widening circles, from the circle of the classroom, school, community, and the world at large.

Most teachers and administrators who read Palmer's book respond at a visceral level to those statements. It may sound corny, but educators go into the profession because of the belief that "teaching is the finest work I know." Is that your belief?

Contained in that ability to make a difference is a moral purpose: "Teaching holds a mirror to the soul" (Palmer, 1998, p. 2). It is important for each of us to understand our beliefs and values because, as Palmer says, "We teach who we are" (p. 2). The more we know about ourselves, the more we can benefit our students because "Good teaching requires self-knowledge: it is a secret hidden in plain sight" (p. 3).

As teachers we ask what we teach, and whom we teach, but less frequently do we ask ourselves the question, "Who is this self that teaches?" Palmer clarified that if one "Reduce[s] teaching to intellect, it becomes a cold abstraction; reduce it to emotions, and it becomes narcissistic; reduce it to the spiritual, and it loses its anchor to the world. Intellect, emotion, and spirit depend on one another for wholeness" (p. 4).

The practice of personal reflection is helpful to each of us as we continue to develop as persons and as professionals, as we try to integrate the intellect, the emotion, and the spirit. Journaling is one way that we can continue to be in touch with who we are and what we believe.

This personal journey is a paradox—the more one looks outward, the more one must look inward to achieve wholeness. The more one reflects personally, the more one must reach out to the outer world to attach meaning to the internal reflections.

As Palmer said, "Teaching [or being an administrator] always takes place at the crossroads of the personal and the public, and if I want to teach well, I must learn to stand where these opposites intersect" (p. 63).

Moral Purpose of the Individual

As the individual reflects on the personal values, one must become conscious of a sense of moral purpose. Fullan (1993) said, "Scratch a good teacher [administrator] and you will find a moral purpose" (p. 10). For most people that can be stated more simply: "Scratch a good teacher [administrator] and there is the desire to 'make a difference.'" There is a need, a desire, a wish to leave the world a better place, a desire to assist teachers, students, and families in the learning process.

Fullan (1993), however, believed that most teachers have this desire but do not act on it enough, that the desire to make a difference lies dormant (p. 13). So, too, is it with administrators. It is not enough to have this wish; it is mandatory that it be acted on by connecting with the larger community in a manner that educates them about the purpose of public education and our responsibility to upcoming generations.

Moral and Ethical Purposes of the Position

The leader must demonstrate ethical leadership. The American Association of School Administrators (AASA) identified five characteristics of ethical leadership:

- Demonstrate ethical and personal integrity
- Model accepted moral and ethical standards in all interactions
- Promote democracy through public education
- Exhibit multicultural and ethnic understanding and sensitivity
- Implement a strategy to promote respect for diversity (quoted in Hoyle, 2002, p. 21)

It is important for each of us to reflect on each of the above statements as to its personal meaning. An ethical leader demonstrates ethical and personal integrity on a daily basis. There are small decisions on a minute-by-minute basis that add up to a role model. The leader exhibits ethical behavior, even if no one is checking on such small things as abiding by copyright laws. Too often access to a photocopy machine makes it too easy to violate copyright laws. An ethical leader does not, and explains to people why an article or book cannot be photocopied wholesale. Instead the leader finds money to purchase a set for classroom use or asks the teachers to find other resources. Or the leader maintains a climate of no gossip. Small things matter, as suggested by the second standard that there are moral and ethical standards in all interactions.

An ethical leader stresses the importance of public education as a way to enhance and rejoice in our democracy. It is important that the voices of the people be heard, whether they are students or parents, just as it is important for all voices to be heard in our country. Having mock elections, hosting student forums and advisories—regardless of the ages of the students—and being a good listener are simple ways to demonstrate and teach about democratic values. It is particularly helpful if the administrator then talks about how these activities are a microcosm of the larger community and how the value of an educated, voting, involved member of our society makes us all richer. It is particularly important to point up the value of differing opinions and discussions. Politics (and education) is messy, but that is a good thing!

It is imperative that administrators be active in voicing their facts and opinions to legislators, rotary groups, chambers of commerce, parent advisory groups, and elsewhere so that the moral purpose of public education remains in the forefront of dialogue. It is not enough to believe; we must act in order to protect the gem of public education that we have in the United States. Anyone who has traveled outside the country, particularly to less developed areas, understands that our system is a treasure and must not be taken for granted. It must be protected, and we must all act as protectors.

Michael Hartoonian, a professor at the University of Minnesota, Minneapolis, gave a keynote speech to a group of social studies teachers in 2003. He told the story of ships on the high seas in the days of wind-powered vessels. As ships met, they asked each other three questions: Who is your captain? What is your cargo? And where are you going?

It is important for us as educators to ask—Who is our captain? What is our cargo? Where are we going? Then, it is important to make that message known.

Education has become increasing political, as members of political parties say they are "education presidents," "education governors," and "education senators." School leaders can no longer afford to sit back. We must all be activists and ethical leaders.

As discussed in the previous chapter on cultural proficiency, to address the fourth and fifth characteristics of an ethical leader, one must create an atmosphere that embraces diversity. Just as the respectful expression of differing opinions is a healthy part of democracy, embracing differing cultures and recognizing the gifts of each makes us all richer human beings.

Summary

Just as for teaching, most people will say they became an administrator to make a difference. The position offers many opportunities to marry knowledge about curriculum and process, to facilitate learning by talking about HOW we learn, to incorporate contemporary knowledge with successes of the past in a manner that makes a difference for all the people we come into contact with. It is a position in which we must embrace a paradox to learn and move forward. Thich Nhat Hanh (1998) described it as a *right action*: "We can protect life, practice generosity, behave responsibly, and consume mindfully" (p. 98).

As ethical administrators, our right actions are rewarded with joy. "If your practice does not bring you joy, you are not practicing correctly" (Hanh, 1998, p. 100). Are you joyful?

Personal Journal

1. Do I feel joy in my work? If so, why? If not, what do I need to do to change?

2. What do I see as my moral purpose in being an educator?

3. How am I taking my energies out into the community to contribute to the discussion about public education?

Group Discussion

1. What is the responsibility of an educational leader and manager to have deeper philosophic discussions about the moral and ethical responsibility of leadership?

2. Is it enough for me to practice ethical and moral leadership, or do I need to facilitate an awareness of it with staff?

14

Balance Between Work and Play

There is no magic recipe for balancing the priorities of work and self, a decision that must be made daily by each individual. However, there are two major questions to ask when trying to establish that balance: What are the needs for a successful 21st-century administrator? What gives the individual administrator joy and peace?

The 21st-Century Administrator

Schools in the 21st century are different. The demands are

- Accountability is more visible, public, and demanding.
- There is an expectation of knowledge of many topics, including technology, diversity, curriculum, and special education.
- There is an expectation of more collaborative leadership. It is expected that the administrator of the 21st century does not close the door but is building teams among staff, parents, and community.
- An administrator must be able to multitask, to juggle competing interests simultaneously.
- An administrator must be an instructional leader.
- An administrator must demonstrate a flexibility and willingness to move forward.

- Administration cannot be shackled to the past but must be willing to use the past to move forward. Sometimes an administrator must make a complete break from the past and do something entirely different.
- An administrator must be interested in the people of the organization, from students to staff to community.

This collaborative, multitasking, people-centered approach is complex yet exhilarating, exhausting yet exciting, rewarding yet exasperating.

What Gives You Joy and Peace?

It is important to marry the needs of the profession with the personal needs of the individual. An unhealthy administrator is of no value to anyone or to any organization. Administrators must be aware of their personal health, emotional health, intellectual health, and spiritual health. It follows logically that a healthy person will be more apt to make healthy choices on all levels and will create an environment that supports such behavior.

Therefore, figure out what is it that gives you joy and peace. Cultivate the opportunity to have that, because joy—and negativity—are contagious.

Each of us has the right to joy, and each of us can create it. We make choices to gather it to us—or not. Joy is not necessarily walking around with a bubbly demeanor. It is the inner glow of peace. It is satisfaction over little things—a student doing well in a class where there had been a struggle, a teacher having a good lesson and feeling good about it, or even a day without major bad behavior by students and no office visits.

Joy is simple and is everywhere. It is recognizing the sunny, windy beautiful day outside as a gift. It is the satisfaction of answering all of your daily e-mails.

It is spending time observing a teacher in a classroom or watching a music performance. Joy can be spending time alone before the start of the school day, simply relishing the sounds and smells of the school.

Joy is internal. Nothing can GIVE you joy. Decide what it is for you and then create situations where you can embrace it. Choose it!

Choice

A balance between work and self is achieved by choice. There are always options, and, consequently, there are always choices. Ultimately, only YOU are responsible for YOU. Neither the district, the teachers, the students, nor your family is responsible for what choices you make.

Choices speak loudly. By choosing to spend a lot of time at work, you have defined your job as more important than other things. By choosing to spend time with students, you have defined the importance of your job as being involved with kids.

With each choice comes a responsibility. A healthy person can recognize the choices and the responsibilities and can enter into that place knowingly and willingly or they can choose to stay away.

It is a helpful phrase to think about the word "should" and "prefer." Many times a person will say, "I *should* finish this project." **Should** implies that there is something external dictating a responsibility. It feels heavy. However, changing the sentence to, "I would *prefer* that I finish the project" shifts the focus of the responsibility to the self. **Prefer** implies a conscious decision to finish the project either now or later. It is an **option** and feels more adult. The person is making a conscious decision as opposed to having some external guilt or nebulous force dictate. Every time you find yourself using the word "should" in your sentence, change it to "prefer" and see how different you feel.

Summary

The 21st-century administrator has a more complex job than ever before. The leader has to know and be able to do more than ever before in a widening circle of public accountability and public scrutiny. It is not just what is good for students; it is how the education system interacts with the larger community.

However, the profession of school administrator or teacher is still one of the most honorable in the world. It is an opportunity to acknowledge the past, work in the present, and prepare for the future. It is an invitation.

Personal Journal

1. Do I have a balance between work and play? If not, what can I do to change it?

2. What benefits do I get from work? What negatives?

3. What benefits do I get from play? What negatives?

4. How can I put the benefits of play and the benefits of work into a healthier balance for me?

Group Discussion

1. Is this a topic that is necessary for an educational leader and manager? Why or why not?

2. What is my comfort level in discussing such a topic?

Peace

Conclusion:
Putting It All Together

A school is a highly intricate organization composed of ideals, missions, and people with a powerful mission of imparting cultural values to our citizens.

Knowing all the theories in the world about effective leadership and the identified traits of an effective leader will not improve student achievement unless the leader is able to manage all the components of the day-to-day and year-to-year operations of a school.

Hopefully, this book will be a support to new and practicing administrators when trying to integrate all the pieces into a synergistic whole that creates what Michael Hartoonian (2003) calls "common wealth," that which we hold in common as part of our cultural infrastructure.

If what Friedman (2005) says is true, that our 21st-century world is flat, we all need to be Hartoonian's "citizens" of a world where educated, responsible adults behave in an ethical fashion to create the type of world we want to live in. Hanh (1998) describes it this way: "Educators, architects, artists, legislators, businessmen—all of us have to come together to create spaces where we can practice peace, harmony, joy, and deep looking" (p. 252). It is that deep looking that is a marriage of leadership, leaders, management, education, ethics, responsibility, and joy. That is the type of world that I would wish for me and for all of you.

References

Abrams, M. H. (Ed.). (1968). *Norton anthology of English literature*. New York: Norton.

Allen, G. W., Rideout, W. B., & Robinson J. K. (1965). *American poetry*. New York: Harper & Row.

Berliner, D. C. (2004, September). *Assessment and public education.* Presented at the 2004 Minnesota Education Summit, Minneapolis, MN.

Bernhardt, V. L. (1998). *Data analysis for comprehensive schoolwide improvement*. Larchmont, NY: Eye on Education.

Bolman, L. G., & Deal, T. E. (2000). *Escape from cluelessness: A guide for the organizationally challenged*. New York: Amacom.

Bolman, L. N. (2000) Re: Is there a correlation between head size and IQ? dSci Network: Neuroscience. Retrieved from http://www.madsci .org/posts/archives/oct2000/970880334.Ns.r.html

Bracey, G. (2000). *Bail me out: Handling difficult data and tough questions about public schools*. Thousand Oaks, CA: Corwin.

Bracey, G. (2003). *On the death of childhood and the destruction of public schools*. Portsmouth, NH: Heinemann.

Brown, J. L. (2004). *Planning and organizing for curriculum renewal* (revised). Alexandria, VA: Association for Supervision and Curriculum Development.

Burns, J. M. (1978). *Leadership*. New York: Harper & Row.

Cambron-McCabe, N., & Cunningham, L. L. (2004, September). Suspending the elephant over the table. *The School Administrator, 61*(9), 16–19.

Carr, J. F., & Harris, D. E. (2001). *Succeeding with standards: Linking curriculum, assessment and action planning*. Alexandria, VA: ASCD.

Carr, M. (2003, November). *Getting your school community to help with public relations*. Principal Advocate Column in *NASSP NewsLeader*. Available from the NASSP Web site.

Carter, J. (2004, November). *History of American presidential campaigns course, McGill University*. Retrieved from http://www.arts.mcgill.ca/ programs/history/faculty/TROYWEB/Courseweb/JimmyCarterThePl ayboyInterview.htm

Chapman, A. (Ed.). (1968) *Black voices: An anthology of Afro-American literature*. New York: New American Library.

Chopra, D. (2002, September). The soul of leadership. *The School Administrator*, pp. 10–12.

Chrisman, V. (2005, February). How schools sustain success. *Educational Leadership, 62*(5), 16–20.

Clark, W. G., & Wright, W. A. (Eds.). (1989). *William Shakespeare: A complete library of his works*. Philadelphia: Running Press.

Collins, J. (2001). *Good to great*. New York: HarperCollins.

Covey, S. R. (1994). *First things first*. New York: Simon & Schuster.

Creighton, T. B. (2001). *Schools and data: The educator's guide for using data to improve decision making*. Thousand Oaks, CA: Corwin.

Cuban, L. (2001) *How can I fix it?* New York: Teachers College Press.

Deal, T. E., & Peterson, K. D. (1999). *Shaping school culture: The heart of leadership*. San Francisco: Jossey Bass.

Delpit, L. (1995). *Other people's children*. New York: New Press.

Dickens, C. *Tale of two cities*. Retrieved from http://www.literature.org/authors/dickens-charles/two-cities/book-01/chapter-01.html

DuFour, R., & Eaker, R. (1998). *Professional learning communities at work: Best practices for enhancing student achievement*. Bloomington, IN: National Educational Services.

Edelman, M. W. (1992). *The measure of our success: A letter to my children and yours*. Boston: Beacon Press.

Eggen, P., & Kauchak, D. (2004). *Educational psychology: Windows on classrooms* (6th ed.). Upper Saddle River, NJ: Pearson.

Evans, R. (2005, April). Reframing the achievement gap. *Kappan, 86*(8), 582–589.

Fiedler, D. J. (2003). *Achievement now: How to assure no child is left behind*. Larchmont, NY: Eye on Education.

Fisher, R., Ury, W., & Patton, B. (1991). *Getting to yes: Negotiating agreement without giving in*. New York: Penguin.

Forsyth, J. (2004, December). Punchback: Answering critics: Does district leadership really matter? *The School Administrator* Web edition. Retrieved from http://www.aasa.org/publications/sa/2004_12/punchback.htm

Forsyth, J., & Turner, J. R. (2005). *Answering the critics of school administration: What are the facts?* Arlington, VA: Educational Research Service.

Frey, P. D., Smart, M. J., & Walker, S. A. (2004). *Standards of practice for teachers: A brief handbook*. Larchmont, NY: Eye on Education.

Friedman, T. L. (2005). *The world is flat: A brief history of the twenty-first century*. New York: Farrar, Straus and Giroux.

Fulghum, R. (1988). *All I really need to know I learned in kindergarten: Uncommon thoughts on common things*. New York: Villard Books.

Fullan, M. (1993). *Change forces: Probing the depths of educational reform*. London: Falmer Press.

Fullan, M. (2002, September). Moral purpose writ large. *The School Administrator,* pp. 14–18.

Garmston, R. J., & Wellman, B. M. (1999). *The adaptive school: A sourcebook for developing collaborative groups*. Norwood, MA: Christopher-Gordon.

Glatthorn, A. A., Carr, J. F., & Harris, D. E. (2004). *Planning and organizing for curriculum renewal*. Alexandra, VA: ASCD.

Glickman, C. D. (1993). *Renewing American's schools: A guide for school-based action*. San Francisco: Jossey-Bass.

Goleman, D., Boyatzis, B., & McKee, A. (2002). *Primal leadership: Realizing the power of emotional intelligence*. Boston, MA: Harvard Business School Press.

Gordon, T. (2003). *T.E.T.: Teacher effectiveness training*. New York: Three Rivers Press

Gould, S. J. (1981). *The mismeasure of man*. New York: Norton.

Gould, S. Jay. (1994, November). Geometer of race. *Discover*, pp. 1–7. Available from http://www.discover.com/issues/nov-4/features/thegeometerofrac441/

Gregory, G. H. (2003). *Differentiated instructional strategies in practice: Training, implementation, and supervision*. Thousand Oaks, CA: Corwin.

Gutin, J. C. (1994, November). End of the rainbow. *Discover*, pp. 71–75.

Hall, G. E., & Hord, S. M. (1987). *Change in schools: Facilitating the process*. Albany: State University of New York Press.

Hanh, T. N. (1998). *The heart of Buddha's teaching*. New York: Broadway Books.

Hancock, M., & Lamendola, B. (2005, March). A leadership journey. *Educational Leadership, 62*(6), 74–78.

Hartoonian, M. (2003, September). *The moral obligation of public education*. Presentation to social studies department, Wayzata High School, Plymouth, MN.

Houston, P. D. (2002, September). Why spirituality, and why now? *The School Administrator*, pp. 6–8.

Hoyle, J. R. (2002, September). The highest form of leadership. *The School Administrator, 59*(8), 18–21.

Jacobs, H. H. (1997). *Mapping the big picture: Integrating curriculum and assessment K–12*. Alexandria, VA: Association of Supervision and Curriculum Development.

James, J. (1996) *Thinking in the future tense: A workout for the mind*. New York: Touchstone.

Kendall, J. S., & Marzano, R. (1997). *Content knowledge: A compendium of standards and benchmarks for K–12 education*. Aurora, CO: Mid-Continent Research and Learning and the Association of Supervision and Curriculum Development.

Kessler, R. (2000). *The soul of education: Helping students find connection, compassion and character at school*. Alexandria, VA: Association of Supervision and Curriculum Development.

Kessler, R. (2002, September). Nurturing deep connections. *The School Administrator*, pp. 22–27.

Killion, J. (2002a). *Assessing impact: Evaluating staff development*. Oxford, OH: NSDC.

Killion, J. (2002b). *What works in the high school: Results-based staff development*. Oxford, OH: National Staff Development Council.

Kubler-Ross, E. (1969). *On death and dying*. New York: Touchstone.

Leadership for student learning: Reinventing the principalship (2004). Retrieved from National Association of Secondary School Principals Web site (http://nasspcms.principals.org/s_nassp/sec.asp).

Lefkowitz, B. (1997). *Our guys*. New York: Random House.

Lindsey, R. B., Roberts, L. M., & Campbell Jones, F. (2005). *The culturally proficient school: An implementation guide for school leaders.* Thousand Oaks, CA: Corwin.

Lindsey, R. B., Robins, K. N., & Terrell, R. D. (2003). *Cultural proficiency: A manual for school leaders.* Thousand Oaks, CA: Corwin.

Lowe, D. (1995). *PowerPoint for dummies.* Foster City, CA: IDG Books Worldwide.

McCauley, C. D. (1990, December). *Effective school principals: Competencies for meeting the demands of educational reform.* Greensboro, NC: Center for Creative Leadership.

McEwan, E. K. (1998). *How to deal with parents who are angry, troubled, afraid, or just plain crazy.* Thousand Oaks, CA: Corwin.

McEwan, E. K. (2003). *10 Traits of highly effective principals: From good to great performance.* Thousand Oaks, CA: Corwin.

McLaughlin, M. J., & Nolet, V. (2004). *What every principal needs to know about special education.* Thousand Oaks, CA: Corwin.

McLeod, S. (2004, October). *Data-driven leadership.* Presentation at Metropolitan Principals' Academy, Minneapolis, MN.

McTighe, J., & Wiggins, G. (2004). *Understanding by design: Professional development workbook.* Alexandria, VA: ASCD.

Marzano, R. (2003). *Classroom management that works.* Alexandria, VA: ASCD.

Marzano, R. (2004). *Building background knowledge for academic achievement.* Alexandria, VA: ASCD.

Minnesota Department of Children, Families & Learning. (1994). *Section 504: Educational Modifications and Accommodations.* St. Paul, MN: Office of Monitoring and Compliance.

Mukhopadhyay, C., & Henze, R. C. (2003, May). How real is race? Using anthropology to make sense of human diversity. *Kappan*, pp. 669–678.

National Association of Secondary School Principals. (2004). *Breaking ranks II: Strategies for leading high school reform.* Reston, VA: Author.

Nickerson, N. (1993). *Secondary School Administrator Course,* University of Minnesota, Minneapolis.

Palmer, P. J. (1998). *The courage to teach: Exploring the inner landscape of a teacher's life.* San Francisco: Jossey-Bass.

Pipher, M. (2002). *The middle of everywhere: Helping refugees enter the American community.* Orlando, FL: Harcourt.

Preuss, P. G. (2003). *Root cause analysis: Using data to dissolve problems.* Larchmont, NY: Eye on Education.

Reagan, T. G., Case, C. W., & Brubacher, J. W. (2000). *Becoming a reflective educator: How to build a culture of inquiry in the schools.* Thousand Oaks, CA: Corwin.

Reeves, D. B. (2002). *Holistic accountability.* Thousand Oaks, CA: Corwin.

Reeves, D. B. (2004). *Accountability for learning: How teachers and school leaders can take charge.* Alexandria, VA: ASCD.

Riche, M. F. (2000, June). America's diversity and growth: Signposts for the 21st century. *Population Bulletin, 55*(2), 13–17, Retrieved from http://www.prb.org/template.cfm?Section=Population_Bulletin1&Template=/PopulationBulletin.cfm

Rosen, L. (2005). *School discipline: Best practices for administrators* (2nd ed.). Thousand Oaks, CA: Corwin.

Rothstein, R. (2004, October). A wider lens on the black-white achievement gap. *Kappan*, pp. 105–110.

Roy, P., & Hord, S. (2003). *Moving NSDC's staff developments standards into practice: Innovation configurations*. Oxford, OH: NSDC.

Saenz, R. (2004) *Latinos and the changing face of America*. Retrieved from http://www.prb.org/

Schmoker, M. (2001). *The results fieldbook: Practical strategies from dramatically improved schools*. Alexandria, VA: ASCD.

Senge, P. (2000). *Schools that learn: A fifth discipline fieldbook for educators, parents, and everyone who cares about education*. New York: Doubleday.

Sergiovanni, T. (2000). *The lifeworld of leadership: Creating culture, community, and personal meaning in our schools*. San Francisco: Jossey-Bass.

Sigford, Jane (1995). *Self-Determinants of Success by the women who are head principals of high schools in Minnesota*. Unpublished doctoral dissertation, University of Minnesota.

Sigford, J. (2005). *Who said school administration would be fun?* (2nd ed.). Thousand Oaks, CA: Corwin.

Silverstein, S. (1974). *Where the sidewalk ends*. New York: HarperCollins.

Slocumb, P. D. (2004). *Hear our cry: Boys in crisis*. Highlands, TX: aha! Process, Inc.

Strauss, W., & Howe, N. (1997). *The fourth turning: An American prophecy*. New York: Broadway Books.

Successful Practices Network. *Process of reforming America's high schools*. [Pamphlet] pp. 16–28. Rexford, NY: Author.

Ury, W. (1991). *Getting past no: Negotiating with difficult people*. New York: Bantam Books.

Using data to improve schools: What's working. (2003). Arlington, VA: American Association of School Administrators.

van Oech, R. (1998). *Whack on the side of the head* (3rd ed.). New York: Warner Books.

Wells, R. (2005). *Ya-yas in bloom*. New York: HarperCollins.

Wheatley, M. J. (1994). *Leadership and the new science: Learning about organization from an orderly universe*. San Francisco: Berrett-Koehler.

Whitaker, T. (1999). *Dealing with difficult teachers*. Larchmont, NY: Eye on Education.

Whitaker, T. (2003). *What great principals do differently: Fifteen things that matter most*. Larchmont, NY: Eye on Education.

Young, P. G. (2004). *You have to go to school—You're the principal! 101 tips to make it better for your students, your staff, and yourself*. Thousand Oaks, CA: Corwin.

Zemke, R., Raines, C., & Filipczak, B. (2000). *Generations at work: Managing the clash of veterans, boomers, xers, and nexters in your workplace*. New York: Amacom.

Zepeda, S. J. (2003). *The principal as instructional leader*. Larchmont, NY: Eye on Education.

Zepeda, S. J. (2004). *Instructional leadership for school improvement*. Larchmont, NY: Eye on Education.

Zmuda, A., Kuklis, R., & Kline, E. (2004). *Transforming schools: Creating a culture of continuous improvement*. Alexandria, VA: ASCD.

Index

**CORWIN
PRESS**

The Corwin Press logo—a raven striding across an open book—represents the union of courage and learning. Corwin Press is committed to improving education for all learners by publishing books and other professional development resources for those serving the field of PreK–12 education. By providing practical, hands-on materials, Corwin Press continues to carry out the promise of its motto: **"Helping Educators Do Their Work Better."**